Bright Ideas
Teacher
Handbooks
Putting on a
Performance

D0620201

For my wife Pauline and our children
Helen, Catherine and Julia.

Published by Scholastic Publications Ltd,
Marlborough House, Holly Walk,
Leamington Spa, Warwickshire CV32 4LS

© 1987 Scholastic Publications Ltd

Author: Peter Morrell
Edited by Jane Hammond
Designed by Dave Cox
Sub-edited by Melissa Bellamy
Photographs by Richard Butchins

Printed in Great Britain by Ebenezer Baylis,
Worcester

ISBN 0 590 70801 5

Front and back covers: photographs by
Richard Butchins

Contents

Contents

Introduction

'A performance – you're thinking of putting on a performance? Why? You must be mad!'

Such may be the reaction of your colleagues to your suggestion.

Of course you're not mad and you must keep telling yourself this so that at least one person believes it – you!

You are, however, concerned with giving children the many and varied experiences that will help to shape their character, develop confidence, heighten their social and co-operative awareness and offer them opportunities for enjoyment and fulfilment, the memories of which may well linger deep into adulthood.

Having successfully overcome slurs on your sanity, and with a deep sense of purpose, you must be realistic about what you are planning to take on. Putting on a performance can be and often is a daunting prospect. You will think, eat, and sleep it 24 hours a day, probably for several weeks.

In putting on a performance you will experience exhaustion, inadequacy, overwork, anger (always contained), frustration, despair, fear, hopelessness, isolation, and acute self-analysis.

Above and beyond all these, however, will be the moments – possibly few and fleeting – when you experience comradeship, sense of purpose, achievement, creativity, enjoyment, a feeling of being needed, satisfaction, anticipation, humour and relief. But perhaps the most rewarding moment in the entire project is when, standing inconspicuously backstage, you watch the children complete the first performance, and realise how they have 'grown' since the project started.

There will be moments, possibly few and fleeting, of comradeship, enjoyment, satisfaction and humour.

Why put on a performance?

Although you have convinced yourself that putting on a performance is possible, you will need to persuade others. You may well find this easier if drama, music and art are all given high priority in the curriculum and there is already integrated work going on. Performances tend to grow more naturally out of such cross-fertilisations and many would maintain that the journey is more important than the destination.

You need to be clear, therefore, in your own mind of the reasons for putting on a performance.

The main reason must surely be the benefits that such a project will bring to the children, the school and you.

The school

The greatest benefits will be achieved if the project involves the whole school. In many schools this is automatic, but in others it has to be worked at and fought for. Benefits include:
- a unifying factor across age groups,
- integrating many curriculum areas,
- bringing staff together to plan and discuss,

- active parental involvement,
- community involvement,
- a staff team effort,
- a further dimension in school-home contact,
- a public relations exercise (a performance will act as a school image-builder and create confidence in the school),
- raising funds,
- raising morale,
- uniting the whole school in a common purpose.

The children

Many of the skills associated with learning will be experienced during the project – manipulative, communicative, oral, social, motor and life skills – all vital in the development of the child. In more detail, the benefit list would include:
- developing memory and retrieval skills,
- developing basic expertise in acting and staging skills,
- communicating with and relating to an audience,

The benefits to the children are enormous – they learn to work as a team and develop self-confidence.

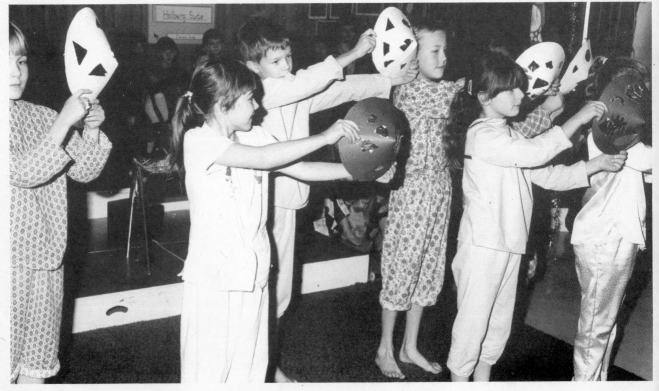

- seeing the performance as many aspects coming together as a whole, not merely 'acting',
- developing clear expression,
- overcoming vocal self-consciousness,
- developing self-confidence and self-discipline,
- developing a co-operative approach,
- feeling an integral part of a team effort working towards a common aim,
- discovering dormant talents and skills,
- giving time and effort for the benefit of others,
- giving pleasure to others,
- gaining satisfaction from doing a good job,
- coping with nerves and pressure,
- organising time to fit in with others,
- developing a love and appreciation of the theatre.

Probably the greatest benefits come from involving all who wish to take part. If the performance is class-based then a part or activity needs to be allocated to every member of the class.

You

Yes, despite everything there are benefits for you:
- developing confidence in working with large numbers of children,
- developing organisational skills,
- developing ways of bringing the best out of people, children and adults,
- raising morale,
- gaining experience,
- gaining enjoyment and satisfaction,
- getting to know the children outside the classroom environment,
- knowing that you have broadened the experiences, opportunities and maybe even the horizons of a group of young people,

All these benefits assume that the performance and the project as a whole are successful, for surely there can be no justification for putting on a performance that is likely to fail.

Having clarified the thinking behind your decision, gain approval from the head, and then be prepared to discuss the many other decisions that need to be made.

Decisions, decisions

Decisions, decisions

INTRODUCTION

BIRMINGHAM POST & MAIL

When children play they often dress up and pretend to be different characters in imaginary situations.

Having made the major decision to put on a performance, you now have a myriad of questions to answer:
- what shall we perform?
- who's going to decide?
- who's going to perform it?
- what resources/facilities are available?
- who's going to help?
- who's going to produce it?
- who will the audience be?

No doubt many more questions, unanswerable at this time, will be fired at you from all quarters. Explain that you had it in mind to discuss that very question with

2

the questioner in the next few days, and that if they've any thoughts on the matter you'd be most interested to hear them. Remember to get back to your 'firing squad' as soon as possible, and also bear in mind that at this point you need support from colleagues in your venture!

What shall we perform?

You have now arrived at what is probably the most difficult part of putting on a performance – choosing the material that will satisfy your criteria. Devote some time to this decision and even when the final decision has been made, be prepared to adapt your choice to suit your school, the children, the staff, the audience, the facilities and the resources.

Basically, you will probably be thinking of either a play or a musical. Within these broad headings, however, there are numerous alternatives.

A play

Written especially for children

A number of publishers are now preparing plays, or books of plays, for use in primary schools, and a browse through their catalogues will help you to identify possibilities, whilst a visit to your music and drama library will give you a selection of what is available locally, and free of charge!

Using a published play can have restrictions and often it is necessary to adapt it to suit your circumstances.

3

Adapted from a book

The method of creating a performance often has its roots in classroom work, for dramatisation of a story or part of a story is an interesting and exciting way of really getting into a book.

There are now numerous published adaptations of children's stories, notably Roald Dahl's *Charlie and the Chocolate Factory*, published by Puffin.

Using a well known and well liked story is a good motivating factor. Teresa, Suzanne, Hilary and Shaun (all aged 11 at the time) had taken part in *Charlie and the Chocolate Factory*, and so enjoyed the experience that they decided to adapt E B White's *Charlotte's Web*. They spent many hours during class time, breaks, lunch hours and at home adapting, refining and redrafting, until they finally presented the completed play – 40 typewritten A4 pages. Next, the four playwrights auditioned their peers for the parts, duplicated the script and arranged rehearsal times.

Time eventually defeated their original plans for the production; instead, they recorded it as a radio play.

The skills, techniques, language and creativity practised in the project were quite considerable.

Improvised drama from stories can be used at many age levels and can provide an excellent basis from which to put on a performance.

Children will often imitate the characters and situations in their reading books as they play, and it would be a natural step for the teacher to organise an extension of this activity.

Popular stories

Stories which have proved popular with a younger age group include:
Topsy and Tim series by Jean and Gareth Adamson,
Meg and Mog series by Helen Nicholl and Jan Pieǹkowski,
Where the Wild Things Are by Maurice Sendak,

BOB BRAY

When children play they often dress up and pretend to be different characters in imaginary situations.

Children will enjoy enacting the hero combat.

Mr Men and Little Miss series by Roger
Hargreaves,
Ladybird/Folk Traditional stories,
stories from reading schemes eg *Village with
Three Corners*,
Roald Dahl stories,
Raymond Briggs stories.

Stories suitable for older primary children
are:
Greek myths and legends,
Norse and Viking legends,
Narnia series by C S Lewis,
Arthur Ransome books,
Silver Sword by Ian Serrailler,
The Hobbit by J R Tolkien,
Alice in Wonderland by Lewis Carroll,
Wind in the Willows by Kenneth Graham.

Shakespearian

Although Shakespeare's plays may well be
outside the experience of primary children
and considered inappropriate by many
primary teachers, there are possibilities.

The plays that are retold in *Favourite
Tales from Shakespeare*, by Bernard Miles,
are lovely to read to children and present
excellent opportunities for discussion,
drama and improvisation, which may even
lead to a performance.

If you are considering Shakespeare,
look for a play which has relevance to the
performers, since it will be easier for the
children to perform with conviction. For
instance, *Romeo and Juliet* and *Hamlet* have
both been successful with primary school
children.

A mummers' play

Very large numbers of mummers' plays
have been collected over the last two
centuries from villages throughout England.
They traditionally have the same
recognisable theme although no two are
exactly alike (see *The Helm Collection*, play
texts collected by Alex Helm).

There are just two basic ingredients:
● they are all traditionally performed at
certain times of the year,
● they contain a death and a resurrection
somewhere in the action.

What is a mummers' play?

Alex Helm, Norman Peacock and E C Cawte, in that authoritative book *English Ritual Drama*, define a mummers' play as 'men's dramatic ceremony', the ceremony being in three fairly distinct categories: the hero-combat, the sword dance ceremony, and the wooing ceremony.

The hero combat is probably the most familiar aspect of the mummers' play, where the two enemies are seen in direct combat. When the villain eventually succumbs, a third character acts as doctor and revives him, hence the death and subsequent resurrection. There is no limit to the number of combats, deaths and resurrections which can occur, so you can easily involve a large number of children. Perhaps your performance will enter the *Guinness Book of Records* as the mummers' play containing the greatest number of deaths and resurrections!

As well as the combat, there are prologues, challenges and counter-challenges, a lament, a cure and the 'quete' included in the hero combat. The quete is usually the final part when money or food is asked for; this can be likened to 'trick or treating' when explaining it to the children.

The sword dance ceremony is a linked sword dance involving no fewer than five men who act together against a single enemy. This could provide an interesting moral issue for discussion, keeping in mind the resurrection!

The wooing ceremony is an aspect of mummers' plays rarely seen outside the East Midlands – more accurately the counties of Nottinghamshire, Leicestershire and Lincolnshire – and involves the wooing of a 'female' by the clown.

The hero-combat ceremony seems to be the most suitable of the three for a school performance.

Traditional elements

The following are traditional elements of the mummers' play to be aware of when planning your performance:
● The seasonal aspect is important. If you plan your performance for the right time of year or, better still, the right day of the year, the greater the authenticity and interest.
● The play comes to or visits the audience, being essentially a travelling ceremony and will often be performed four or five times each evening (usually in pubs nowadays). When Britain was a more agricultural society, the plays were taken from house to

MICK HAND

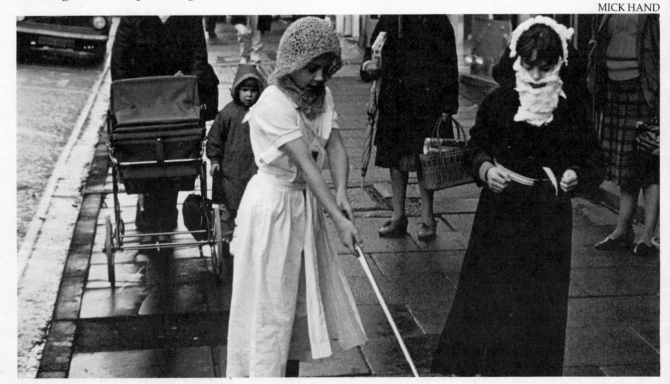

The sword dance ceremony is also very popular.

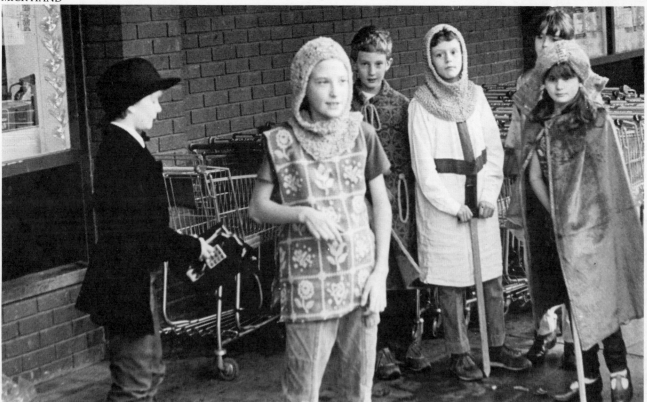

Costumes for mummers' plays are often a mixture of styles from different periods.

house or farm to farm. This is when the 'quete' became an important element, because money, food or ale would be asked for at each destination, with predictable consequences as the evening wore on!
● The play is short, usually no longer than half an hour, so your performance would need to be part of a festival of mummers' plays, or a performance that includes a mummers' play as one aspect.
● The staging is simple – merely a circle which is first described by the players. The size of the circle will depend upon where the play is being performed but there needs to be a defined performing area, which could be within a circle formed by the audience.

Defining the performing area can become the initial part of the play. The performers may enter one by one, walking around in a circle, or the presenter may walk round the circle. In some plays, the 'female' enters with a broom and 'sweeps' the audience back to define the circle!
● Performing a traditional mummers' play is exclusively a male activity, but I have seen mummers' plays performed most successfully with girls; in fact, one of the

girls was disguised as a male playing the 'female'!
● A fairly bold, declamatory style of vocal presentation has become traditional, perhaps due to the fact that the performers are untrained actors. Originally there were no words or script, and the performance was a ritual action. Many varieties of vocal presentation occur. In the Ripon (Yorkshire) Sword Play, the mummers stand in a straight line and speak at the tops of their voices with no inflection. In others, the words merely form a skeleton for improvisation. It is worth remembering, though, that in the mummers' play, action rules – OK!

Costume

Costume tends to depend upon two things: the troupe who perform the play and the play itself.

Many characters suggest costume by their name, but it is worth remembering that disguise is the key, and often a character's costume will comprise items from different historical periods.

The Marshfield Paper Boys use masses of shredded paper to effect disguise. This

7

starts at the top of the conical head-dress and shoulders, falling all the way down the body.

A puppet play

Here is your chance to produce something entirely different, for puppetry enables you and the children to create a new dimension. It can be entirely original and caters for the whole primary age range.

Presenting puppets is essentially a co-operative effort and can involve children, operators, voices, announcer, musicians, stage manager, props, curtain, sound effects, set designers, set constructors, scenery, costume and puppet makers. It is also a good way of including children who do not want to act but are happy to participate anonymously behind the scenes.

A puppet play brings in the added dimensions of puppet-making and the skill of puppetry.

Making puppets

A puppet presentation will need careful planning, and will probably be part of a wider topic which will include making puppets. 'Movement' as a topic heading could well include puppetry, having first investigated how human limbs work and having tried to construct limb movements with card and brass fasteners.

Designing and constructing marionettes or rod puppets would develop naturally but don't make designs too complicated, especially for younger children, whose dexterity and concentration span require results sooner rather than later.

Over-complicated puppets will produce not only considerable design and construction problems, but also restrictions in performance.

Let the children explore the movement possibilities, remembering that puppets can do things that people can never hope to do, and have shapes that people hope they will never develop. Gigantic noses, five legs, and heads that lift off bodies and then return, will often suggest scripts and dialogues. If it's your first show, plan something simple but effective and do it well. Such success creates positive attitudes, and the children will probably want to present another play almost immediately!

8

Children can manipulate hand puppets very easily, making them sing, dance, and even die dramatically.

The type of puppet you choose needs to be matched to the children's stage of development.

In *The Puppet Theatre Handbook*, Marjorie Batchelder sets out the many possible varieties.

Shadow puppets

Shadow puppets, probably the oldest type of puppet, originated in the Far East and are flat figures operated by rods or wires against a screen which is illuminated from behind. Perhaps the most familar is a silhouette of black cardboard mounted on a stick or wire. They are quick to make and easy to use, operated usually from below.

Hand puppets

Hand puppets may be finger or glove puppets, using the thumb and third (or little) finger for the hands or arms, and the forefinger for the head. This type of puppet can pick up objects, fight, dance, sing and even die in a most dramatic fashion. They can also move quickly and easily and are not too difficult to make.

Children designed and made these simple hand puppets.

9

Hand and rod puppets

Hand and rod puppets are similar to hand puppets but the arms are longer and jointed at the shoulder and elbow, and they are controlled by rods from below. They allow for a greater variety of hand movements but are less dexterous at picking up objects.

Rod puppets

Rod puppets are operated from below by a metal or wooden rod which acts as a central control. The head and hands are usually controlled by lighter rods. The puppets can be a variety of sizes and shapes, but always bear in mind the overall weight.

Marionettes

Marionettes or string puppets are controlled by strings and operated from above. They are generally more difficult to construct and control because the operator is further from the puppet. They can perform a wide variety of movements and are the logical development of a 'Movement' topic.

Points to consider

● Scale is important. If you are using scenery, try to make it to the same scale as the puppets eg for one quarter life-sized puppets, other effects should be to quarter scale (except, of course, where exaggeration is important to the plot).
● Go for simplicity.
● Plan the performance before making scenery etc. Construction of a good, relevant set can take much time and effort and it would be disappointing, even demoralising, to make something that is not needed in the performance.
● Decide whether the puppet heads will be carved, modelled, or made from odds and ends. This will often depend on what resources and facilities are available to you. Materials that can be used are potatoes, apples, swedes (watch the weight factor), balls (tennis, ping-pong, rubber), beads, wooden spoons, paper cups, gourds, paper bags, papier mâché, sawdust and paste, Plasticine, clay, plaster of Paris in moulds (quite a complicated process), or wood (softwood – balsa, pine; hardwood – walnut, mahogany).

10

● When modelling or making puppet faces have lots of masks handy, for the puppet's face is a 'mask', a motionless expression, unlike a human actor who can change expression. The face will therefore be an integral part of the puppet's personality and character.
● A very simple marionette can be made from a stocking filled with toy stuffing, and weighted in the hands, feet and lower trunk.
● Be sure to allow lots of time for the children to experiment, practise and master the movements of the puppets. Poorly handled puppets will spoil any performance!

Revue or variety show

These are probably the least complicated type of performance to produce but often the least successful in terms of achieving your aims in putting on a performance.

Essentially they comprise separate, often individual, acts. This has its

These rod puppets were also made by children.

Rehearsals are less complicated for a variety show, and if someone drops out, the show still goes on.

advantages, in that if someone drops out the show can go on, and the rehearsal schedule tends to be less complex. However, it may not give the participants the co-operative feeling and sense of collective achievement of other types of performance.

As its name suggests, variety is the key to a variety show, and the more variety you can include the better. However, there are limits as to the range of acts that primary school children will offer: eight 'pop' groups miming to current hit records, a magician who hasn't quite mastered the disappearing coin trick, and the impressionist who can only 'do' Michael Crawford saying 'Betty' don't constitute a variety show in the eyes of an adult-dominated audience!

Two approaches

A revue can be approached from two viewpoints:
● The dictionary definition of revue – 'a loosely constructed play or series of scenes or spectacles presenting or satirising current

events' – is an adult concept and should be avoided. For children to try to create adult humour for an adult audience is not in the true spirit of primary education. This type of revue needs to be highly organised and drilled so that acts appear at exactly the right moment, and the continuity jokes and sketches need to be funny and not embarrassing.
● The second, more appropriate type of revue comprises a series of scenes linked together by a common theme. This tends to give the revue more shape and purpose.

You will need to choose the theme carefully, for it needs to provide the stimulus for a considerable number of items, maybe ten to fifteen.

Draw up a flow diagram so that you can see what possibilities your theme presents. Ask the children to draw up a similar type of diagram, for they will often see a theme from a different point of view. Following discussion, an agreed series of items may form the skeleton of your revue.

A musical

If you mention an end-of-term performance, most people would probably think of singing, acting, instrumental accompaniment and dancing – a musical show. Following the primary school traditions of integrated curriculum and class teacher approach, a performance would be the combination of a number of aspects, particularly words and music. Such a performance will allow you to involve more easily all the children who volunteer.

An existing show

How many shows can you think of in, say, a minute? *West Side Story, Oklahoma, Jesus Christ Superstar, 42nd Street, Oliver, Cats, Cabaret, South Pacific* . . . . Ask the children how many of them have been to a show, how many have bought records or cassettes of shows, what their favourite show is and why, and which show they would like to have had a part in.

If you choose an existing show, the audience and possibly some of the participants may already have concepts of the show which have developed from their own experiences. They may have seen a professional performance, heard the record or cassette, or seen a film. It would be inappropriate to ask children of primary school age, using primary school facilities and resources, to be subjected to comparison with the sophisticated productions of modern theatre. It might also be inappropriate to expect audiences to keep reminding themselves that 'they're only children'.

Oliver

There are shows, however, which have been successfully adapted and performed by primary school children; perhaps one of the more feasible is *Oliver*, since children can 'play' children, many of the songs are probably known to the participants, and costumes of that period are generally quite easy to find (you will need a competent pianist to make the accompaniment come alive).

HMS Pinafore

Gilbert and Sullivan operas have also been successfully produced in primary schools. With nine-, ten- and eleven-year-olds, including a chorus of more than 120 children who were on stage throughout the performance, plus the main characters. Other children made, painted, and shifted the scenery, operated the lights, and took on front-of-house duties, involving in total more than 150 children.

Obviously, a work such as *HMS Pinafore* is not suitable for primary school children as written, and must be adapted. The octet and chorus 'Farewell My Own' is a good example of the need for adaptation. Since some of the staff in this case were familiar with the work, the task of adapting it to the abilities of the children and the resources of the school was relatively quick and easy.

Joseph

Perhaps the most notable show that has been performed in primary schools is *Joseph and the Amazing Technicolour Dreamcoat*, which was originally written as a children's cantata in the late 1960s, and was first performed in London in May 1968.

Following its recording and subsequent performance in St Paul's Cathedral, *Joseph* has been added to and extended into a full length stage show with adults taking lead parts. It remains a favourite, and is equally effective as a cantata for soloists and chorus, or as a full stage show.

Joseph remains one of my favourites, too, for it was my first attempt at putting on a performance.

I felt it had a great deal to offer young people: catchy, well written melodies, witty lyrics, and a vibrancy and excitement that I had not previously experienced in music for schools. It was arguably the first work of a new era of music for schools and remains, in my opinion, one of the very best.

Cantata

There must be literally hundreds of cantatas amongst the publishers' catalogues to choose from. This choice will narrow as you list your criteria:
● linked to a topic,
● Biblical context,
● period in history,
● fable/folktale/fairy story/legend,
● time of year eg Christmas,
● number of voices available,

A number of existing musical shows can be adapted to be performed successfully by children.

A cantata may be adapted or written for primary school chorus and orchestral or other instrumental parts.

- possible soloists,
- range of voices,
- proficiency of musicians.

Originally, a cantata was a mixture of aria and recitative for one voice, but today those cantatas which take a Biblical or other sacred theme are more in the style of a small-scale oratorio, complete with choruses and often with orchestral or instrumental parts for primary school use.

No need for scenery

One strong advantage, especially if this is your first performance, is that it will work successfully without scenery or effects.

This brings to mind a performance of the cantata *Guy of Warwick*. We had performed it many times as a straight cantata, but on this particular occasion we were invited to perform it during the Warwick Arts Festival in the grounds of Warwick Castle. What a magnificent backdrop – the castle ramparts, with Guy's Tower looming majestically behind 50 children as they sang:
'Down by the banks of the Avon River
There stands a town of some fame,
A castle with turrets and huge, grey towers,
One bears our hero's name . . .'

Where scenery and effects are not used, the performers become both the aural and visual scenery, and you will need to consider how the staging and costume could

maximise the effect. You will also need to work hard to attain the best possible clarity of words in the performance, for often the words will be the only way for the audience to follow the story.

The dramatic backdrop of Warwick Castle.

14

Operetta

An operetta is, as you would expect, a short opera where the dialogue can be spoken as well as sung.

Here you will need scenery and probably effects, but operetta is an exciting area and one to which primary school children will respond positively, given the right build-up and introduction.

Gilbert and Sullivan operettas are among the more lasting examples, and *HMS Pinafore* was suggested earlier.

A successful project

Some schools, in conjunction with the Royal Opera House (Covent Garden), have been involved in writing and performing their own operetta. Bishop's Tachbrook CE Combined School, near Leamington Spa, was one such school. Lesley Funge and Jo Simpson, the project leaders, relate the basic ideas, the practical developments and their own experiences of putting on an operetta:

'The project began with the formation of a theatre company, Star Enterprises, and involved about 30 children, aged from nine to twelve years. Each child held at least one responsible position in the company and was expected to make a full contribution to the final production. There were designers to create the set and costume sketches, painters, carpenters and electricians to bring the scenery to life, a wardrobe department to make and maintain the costumes, production managers to oversee practical construction, stage managers to deal with those on stage and a director to run rehearsals.

'A musical director was in charge of music practices whilst a make-up department added the finishing touches. The administrative personnel advertised the project and the production through posters, letters, telephone calls and press releases, and dealt with invitations and tickets. Finally, at least nine of the company were chosen as actors. All the jobs were allocated through auditions held at the outset of the project.

'The script had been constructed by a group of writers during months of questions, answers and discussion, following guidelines suggested by the project originators.

'Looking back, we feel it was a

HEART OF ENGLAND NEWSPAPERS

An operetta is an exciting and enjoyable project for the children.

worthwhile and successful project. The effect on the development of our children has been varied and, on the whole, very positive. Many were able to grow and mature through their work and they certainly learned a great deal about responsibilities attached to real company jobs.

'Many also learned a sensitivity towards others and a spirit of helpfulness which grew out of the corporate feelings embodied in the project. The children were determined to see the project through and reaped great satisfaction from being given the freedom to try things out, discuss problems and complete practical work in an area which was new, exciting and real.'

Reasons for success

Star Enterprises Company presented *The Anciento Enigma* to an awed and appreciative audience of 200 eight- to twelve-year-olds at our school. Their concentration and interest were held throughout the performance. None of the 'I'm becoming bored' or 'I've switched off' signs were evident.

There are a number of possible reasons for this. Our children were aware that everything they saw and heard had been organised by children. They could see the lighting and sound technicians at work around them, and were aware that the two teachers who accompanied the Star Enterprises Company were part of the audience, and were taking no part whatsoever in the performance. The entire company displayed great commitment and dedication to the task of putting on a performance, and a professionalism that our children really admired.

The spontaneous and long-lasting applause that greeted the curtain call was richly deserved. This was an ambitious yet fascinating project and one that fulfilled many of the reasons for putting on a performance.

A masque

The masque is by no means a new idea, for in Shakespeare's time the English court was enjoying musical festivities linked to many celebratory events through the medium of the masque.

But what is a masque? Basically, it is a dramatic presentation which includes music, songs, poetry, dialogue and dance, taking as its theme or message an item of topical importance. So, in producing a masque, you will be looking for the integration of these different art forms, the musical input being a central feature.

Decide on the theme or message through discussion with the children. Then, depending upon their age and abilities, they may well be able to write the script, compose the songs and music, and design and make the scenery and costumes.

I have found that themes suggested by the children vary considerably from 'soccer' to 'sex equality', but the recurring, popular themes are 'nuclear war', 'famine' and 'space'. It is quite possible to weave all these themes into one presentation.

Children will respond positively to this type of performance because, basically, it involves their ideas and work.

Old-time music hall

This seems to be quite a popular choice of project for putting on a performance and it has much to commend it. Like a variety show, a music hall show comprises a number of separate items, linked by a Victorian or Edwardian theme which can be

JOHN WALMSLEY

The Anciento Enigma held the children's attention.

A masque involves many different art forms based on a theme – a good opportunity to include dance.

rehearsed individually, only coming together quite near the performance date. In practical terms, this means you don't need to begin whole school rehearsals during the third week of September for a Christmas performance.

Like a variety show, a music hall show can have the disadvantage of becoming too individualistic or class/group-based, making the feeling of a co-operative effort harder to achieve.

Why not therefore include whole company items, such as a medley of old-time songs accompanied by the music hall band, and invite the audience to join in?

Master of Ceremonies

You will, of course, need a Master of Ceremonies (complete with hammer) or, better still, two Masters – a boy and girl to keep each other company in front of a large, noisy audience. Two can also share the workload and play comic and straightman between items. Theirs is a most important role, for the pace and continuity of the performance depend to a large degree upon them, so take your time selecting the most suitable children.

The band

The music hall band is also a must, and the children concerned will very much enjoy and appreciate being an essential part of the performance. Place the band on stage so that they both feel and look an integral part. Give them their own 'spot' – an item specially selected for them to show their prowess – and of course the band is invaluable when sound effects or mood music is required.

Dressing up the band for a music hall show provides an ideal opportunity to involve period costume. If parents and friends of the school attend such performances in costume too, it really makes the occasion come alive and is a tremendous boost to the children.

Choosing the items

The content of your music hall show will depend on your children, resources and facilities, but may include:
● old-time songs,
● monologues eg 'Albert and the Lion', 'Green Eyed Yellow Idol' etc.
● instrumental items,
● mummers play,

17

Children rehearse a sing-along medley – an essential ingredient for an old-time music hall finale.

- magician/ventriloquist,
- sand dance,
- gymnasts/strongman act/jugglers,
- shadow theatre.

You will need to discuss and agree your list of items quite early, and you will need to know their approximate timings. Your script for the Master of Ceremonies will only fit together when you know the running order of the show, for their task is to maintain continuity and introduce various items. Try to balance the programme so that each act is a contrast to the previous one. Open the evening with a rousing song and finish the show with a sing-along medley, so that the audience will go home feeling a part of the show.

I have always found a very positive reaction from both participants and audience towards an old-time music hall, as it provides a great deal of fun and enjoyment.

Pantomime

Pantomimes give scope for a wide variety of content and lend themselves to local as well as school references. Teachers' names in place of traditional ones are highly popular with children, who will be most keen to typecast teachers, dinner ladies and the caretaker in key parts! The local pub often gets a mention in the script, along with the shoe shop in *Cinderella*, the garden centre in *Jack and the Beanstalk*, and a cat food advertisement in *Dick Whittington*. The local council, bus service, prices in the shops, traffic congestion, roadworks, all deserve the pantomime treatment.

Pantomimes provide numerous opportunities for involving large numbers of children, the whole school in some cases, often bringing a keen sense of togetherness and co-operation across a wide age and ability range.

Traditional elements

Although pantomime has seen considerable metamorphosis over the centuries, traditions have developed and become essential parts of the performance. Some you may be able to incorporate if pantomime is your choice.

All the characters should be clearly defined and contrasts should be extreme. Villains must be really evil so that the audience feels justified in booing and hissing. Traditionally, the villain enters stage-left (ie the audience's right) whilst the good fairy enters stage-right (ie the audience's left), based on the idea that good sits on the right hand of God in the old miracle plays.

Colours, too, are important. In early times, Harlequin was dressed in a suit made of brightly coloured silk diamonds – yellow for jealousy, blue for faithfulness to

Columbine, scarlet for anger and black for invisibility – and pointed to them at the appropriate moment in the play.

The principal girl and boy (always played by a girl) appear last in the finale, and the original tradition was for the principal girl to deliver the final couplet (called the 'tag'). This is not always adhered to today.

'Break a leg' replaces 'good luck' as the wish for a successful performance whilst it is considered a lucky omen if, on the opening night, an actor trips on his first entrance!

The props should be larger than life – enormous combs or keys, etc.

The audience expect to take part in a pantomime.

Involving the audience

The audience must be your prime consideration, for a pantomime is essentially family entertainment where the children in particular are expecting a faithful representation of their favourite bedtime stories. Adults, too, have preconceived ideas of what pantomime should be: ie straightforward, traditional, and larger-than-life entertainment.

Involve your audience – they are expecting it. 'Oh no he isn't!' prompts them to respond with 'Oh yes he is!' and, of course, whenever the audience is asked about a character's whereabouts, their reply is 'Behind you!' There may be TV catch-phrases which could be used, such as 'Hi de hi' and 'I shall say zis once' (spoken in the appropriate 'French' accent), to which the audience replies 'and only once'. But don't let your pantomime develop into a catalogue of impressions. That is for revue, and requires a different audience reaction.

A pantomime will usually include an audience participation song. Place it near the end when the audience feels it's now or never, as far as singing is concerned!

The role of music

The music should, above all, take the story or plot forward. Don't include popular, chart-topping songs unless they fit in with the story. They can interrupt the flow, change the atmosphere and spoil the illusion. Try the 'half-and-half' approach, using well known melodies but writing your own relevant words, to help the story to move forward.

The 'half-and-half' approach is not new, of course, for it was used by the characters of the *commedia dell'arte* in the sixteenth century, who entertained the French at the big Paris fairs of Saint Germain and Saint Laurent. Their pantomimes were of a farcical nature and often quite earthy. Music only appeared as small snatches of well known melodies with occasional lyrics. Through the centuries more was made of this idea, until songs developed consisting of a refrain for the chorus and couplets for the individual singer. In this form, they became known as 'vaudevilles'.

There must be literally hundreds of well known singable tunes waiting to be revived with different words. Some may need transposing into a key within the vocal range of the children but many can be used as they are. Of course, you will need to check copyright restrictions with the publisher first.

Characters in pantomime are clearly defined – villains looking evil and the good fairy dressed in white.

Theme tunes

Just as pantomime songs can be helpful in furthering or reinforcing the story-line, so a theme tune can be most useful during scene-changes, or for developing a different mood. For example, in the pantomime *Jackie and the BEANSTALK Game* (by Elizabeth Chapman and Peter Morrell, published by Scholastic Publications in *Junior Education*, October 1986), 'Jackie's Theme' can be used on many occasions.

A theme tune will also create a sense of calm during those rare occasions when something goes wrong, and an otherwise lengthy pause would spoil the continuity. Balance and judgement must be used to decide how often the theme tune appears, for over-exposure will create a negative response from the audience, such as, 'Oh not *that* tune again!', or 'Can't they play anything else?'

Remember to give the good fairy and the wicked villain their own short theme, just enough to accompany their entrances and to focus the audience's attention. A few glissandos on a glockenspiel for the fairy, or some heavy bass notes on a xylophone, cello or piano for the villain will suffice.

The pantomime animal

Finally, there's that old favourite, the pantomime animal. Depending upon what costume is available, you may have to adapt the script to accommodate it. It might be a horse or a cow – one school used a blackbird which now appears in almost every show, with a part written especially for it, yet keeping within the general story. The reason was that a parent had made the costume so beautifully that it seemed a pity to use it just a couple of times. So, every year it is taken carefully out of its packing-case and given to some extremely appreciative child who feels proud to be the blackbird.

Essentially, then, a pantomime should be entertaining for all the family, a chance to sit back, enter into all the old traditions, and go home feeling better for the experience.

In the words of an old pantomime bill:
'Three things are required at Christmas time,
Plum pudding, beef and pantomime.
Folks could resist the former two;
Without the latter none could do.'

Pantomime wouldn't be complete without the pantomime animal. It could be any kind of animal – a horse, a bird, or even an imaginary creature designed and made by the children.

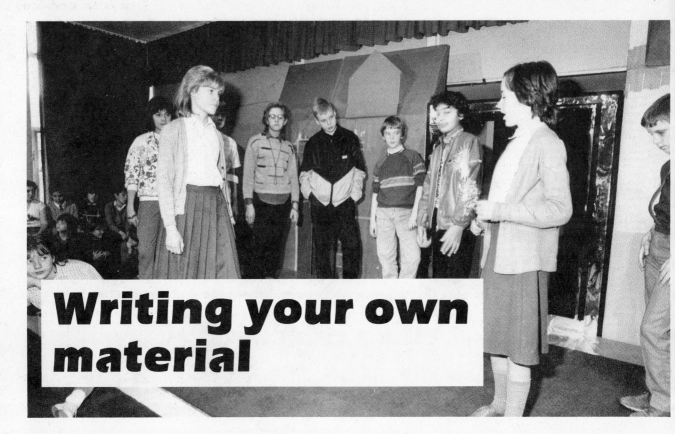

Writing your own material

You may have reached this point still feeling doubtful about putting on a performance. Perhaps you are attempting to incorporate a large chorus, a competent boy soprano whose voice could break any day, 23 descant recorders, five small keyboards, one mouth-organ (not very well played by a keen nine-year-old), vast supplies of ageing, untuned percussion instruments, and three shepherds' costumes (small). In this case, the performance must be original, if not unique!

Above all, it should be relevant to the children who will be performing it. The great advantage of writing your own material is that it will be tailor-made for your school and what you hope to achieve by putting on a performance.

You will probably be looking for up to ten soloists and a large chorus, although you may feel that soloists are not needed. You may think that it is of greater educational benefit to have more children playing smaller parts, rather than a few playing large parts.

Do try to avoid the performance that involves lots of children who wait in a room down the corridor for half an hour, present their one-liner and return to the room for the remainder of the performance. It would be better to have a large chorus who are an integral part of the action, or groups who can appear a number of times.

Choosing your approach

Once you have made this decision, choose the approach you will take:
● an historical episode,
● a local folk or historical tale,
● a well known folk hero or tale,
● adapting a story that you have worked on in class,
● an aspect of topical importance, such as conservation, space or famine,
● an area of curriculum,
● a moral issue.

A local folk or historical tale

If a local folktale is chosen you will need to write, adapt or rewrite the story-line and match it to the children and your school situation.

You may well find conflicting versions and must decide which best suits your school's performance.

This situation occurred during my research into the story of *Guy of Warwick*. I unearthed six accounts of Guy's life, describing his heritage, travels and adventures. These accounts fell roughly into two contrasting stories.

The conflicting versions of Guy's story became an interesting discussion point with the children and developed into the more generalised question of legends – how true are they? We talked about the period in history when Guy lived, about 1,000 years ago. What was the state of newspapers, radio, and television in those days? How would news travel? How long would news take to travel? How many people would be involved in relaying the story? If it was written down at the time, who would have written it? What language would have been used?

The tale of Guy produced a considerable amount of written evidence but it may be necessary, with some folktales, to add your own interpretation to a story that has been passed on, largely by word of mouth.

A well known folk hero or tale

Well known folktales and traditional stories can be found in numerous publications. Fairy tales, fables, and adventure stories all have story-lines which can be quite easily adapted. It is important to check copyright restrictions and whether your chosen tale is still in copyright. It may well be that your tale forms part of a collection – again, check that no infringements are made.

If you decide to adapt a traditional tale, check the publisher's catalogue, since a change of title may be required. This happened to a school who adapted the story of Lady Godiva, only to find that there was already a publication called *Lady Godiva*. Some quick thinking changed their title to 'How to Catch Cold Whilst Riding a Horse through the Streets of Coventry'. But that didn't quite fit into the five-syllable pattern essential for the opening song, so they changed it to 'Coventry Lady'.

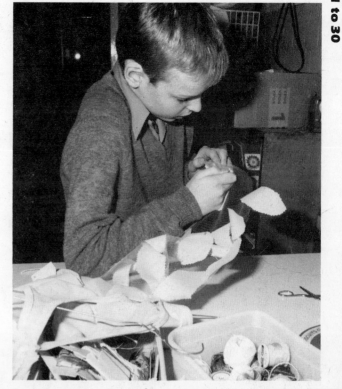

Every child will have a part to play in the project.

Developing a story in class

You may choose not to present a complete, finished article to the children, but decide upon a plot and then work with the children to fill in the details.

'The Great Beefburger Racket' began life like this. It was to be a homely tale about the Northenders led by Greasy Sam, and the Southenders led by Fats Poloni. The action took place somewhere in America and was about the rivalry between two 'muncheasies' (fast-food emporiums) which eventually sold out to Donald MacRonald for a lifetime's supply of properly cooked beefburgers! The children were involved in improvising dialogue, composing musical interludes, and designing and making props, scenery and costumes. Their commitment and enthusiasm came across throughout the whole performance.

An alternative but similar method would be to draw up a list of scenes and again work with the children to decide upon the details. This way of writing your own material will be easier to achieve if drama or an integrated arts approach are part of your curriculum.

Factors affecting your decision

Whoever decides on the type of performance needs to be a totally involved member of the production, the 'absentee landlord' type of decision-maker can only lead to problems.

The decision may involve any of the following: headteacher; music co-ordinator; English/language co-ordinator; interested staff; children; all staff; a combination of one or more.

Who is going to perform it?

You will need to take into account the age of the children who will be performing, and their concentration span; their ability to learn words, sing (vocal range), play instruments, act, improvise, taking on other areas of responsibility and how they work with others; the size of the group (class, year group, whether to use half or all of the school) and girl/boy balance.

Are the children used to performing, or will this performance be a new experience for them?

What resources are available?

classrooms
hall
staging
lighting
assembly areas
props
scenery
audio-visual
seating
exit notices (illuminated?)
blackout
rehearsal time (timetabled or extra-
    curricular)
make-up
instruments
financial budget

Who is going to help?

staff (teaching and non-teaching)
parents

24

local community
children
ex-pupils/parents/staff
friends of the school
advisory teachers
peripatetic teachers
local theatre/drama group
colleagues in neighbouring schools

Who is going to produce it?

In many schools, the producer will be either the head, the music co-ordinator or the language co-ordinator, whilst in others it could be any member of staff whose interest, enthusiasm and commitment lie in this area. There is no reason why it should be just one person, but the important message is that those involved must be able to get on with each other.

If the performance is based on original material written within the school, then it is sensible for the authors and composers to produce it. Sharing the work-load would also seem sensible, especially in a musical where one person can oversee the musical input, whilst another looks after the acting.

Occasionally, a situation may arise which wasn't planned but works out extremely well. A colleague producing a music–drama was within two weeks of the performance when his co-producer had to withdraw. The husband of a helper offered assistance, and a new partnership quickly developed. Not only did this 'blessing in disguise' carry out the co-producer's role superbly, but he also became more heavily involved in subsequent performances by writing a number of scenes. Perhaps there's someone nearer than you think, just waiting to be asked!

Who will the audience be?

The audience could be from one specific category or a combination, including children (older, younger or of a similar age), adults, children from another school, the elderly, or the handicapped.

You may decide to take your performance on tour, visiting neighbouring schools, play groups, old people's homes and day centres. This will need to be planned from the outset of the project.

If the show is written especially for the school, the author should ideally produce it.

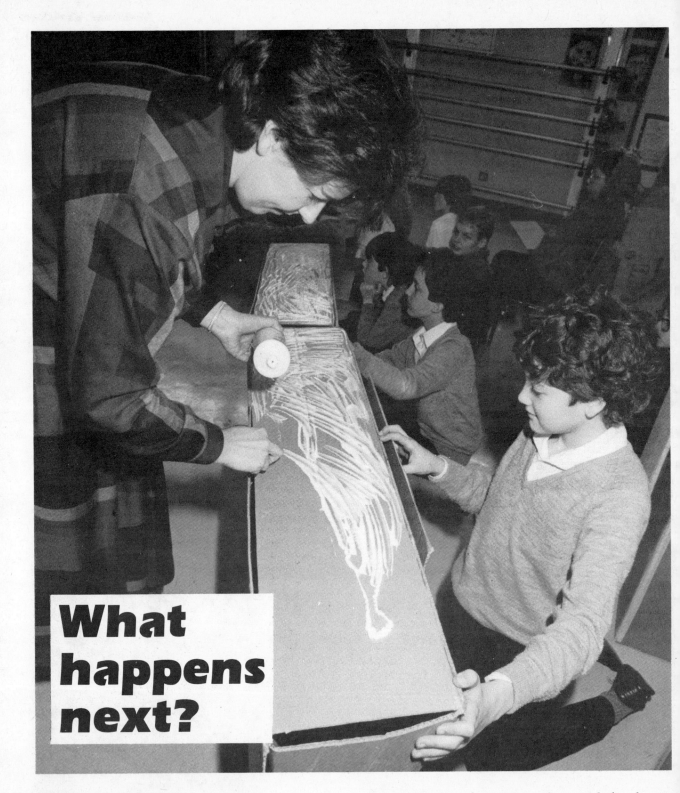

What happens next?

Break the news

There is a great deal of planning and organisation to be done, but before you can sit down to seriously consider those aspects, you need to communicate your final decision. Break the news that in 'x' weeks' time there will be a performance.

This is a crucial stage, so be prepared to sell, enthuse about, and even defend your decision.

There may well be colleagues who are not particularly overjoyed at the prospect of putting on a performance, suggesting that such activities are peripheral and take up too much class time. There may even be those who say it disrupts the whole school and it's just not worth the bother.

Who to involve

Try to involve colleagues at an early stage, and ask them how they think they might be able to help, even if it means employing a little flattery.

In a small school, the whole staff will most probably have been involved in the initial discussions, and the team will be self-motivating from an early stage.

In larger schools this may not happen at first, and you need to decide on the minimum number of staff required to put on your performance.

Decide which areas need covering, then you can ask specific members of staff to take on a particular area. This, of course, will greatly depend on your choice of material, but the following areas need consideration:
● music, acting, choreography, and costume,
● advertising, administration and finance,
● special effects/sound, scenery and lighting,
● parental involvement and refreshments.

It could be that only some of these areas are relevant to your performance, but it would be most useful at this stage if 'volunteers' could be found to take charge of these aspects. It will certainly take a considerable burden off your shoulders to know that Muriel is looking after scenery and Clive has agreed to work on the choreography.

You may even find that, as the project gains momentum and tangible results begin to appear, more colleagues will offer help and/or advice. If you can gain more converts this time, it will be easier next time, so find them a job as soon as possible.

Material to distribute

Give each member of staff a brand new folder with the name of your performance and their name in bold letters on the front, and a copy of the material neatly arranged inside.

Distribute a sheet of 'decisions so far', including the main, relevant details and who's responsible for what, and pin one on the staffroom notice-board. It would be useful to have a notice-board placed centrally in the school, for the children to refer to as well.

You will need a copy of the material for each staff helper, as well as the main characters. This may involve expense if

Find colleagues who are willing to take charge of costumes and the many other aspects of your production.

copies have to be bought or are legally photocopiable. Some publications now state that photocopying of material is permissible – always check this first.

Draw up a budget

Have you spoken to the head about a financial budget? It is wise to agree an amount at the outset so that you can budget for the various areas. A budget checklist appears on page 147.

Sponsorship

What about sponsorship? For many schools it is taboo, but some firms have local funds set aside for use in fostering links and good relationships with the local community. Also, local traders will often be happy to make a donation towards a specific project. A mention in the programme of organisations which have 'kindly made donations' will usually suffice.

Self-financing

If sponsorship from outside school is deemed inappropriate, you may have to think of other ways to raise funds. Hopefully, you will manage to recoup this outlay from money raised by the performance, but you will need a float from the very outset for necessary expenses. It will be a tremendous help in your planning and your credibility if you can budget for the whole project to be self-financing. This could be an area for a colleague to oversee because, depending upon the scale of your performance, it could be a very time-consuming aspect.

Fund-raising

Often the children will be keen to suggest ways of raising funds and organising events, such as a disco, second-hand book sale, second-hand toy sale, sponsored event, or jumble sale.

This is a good opportunity to involve parents at an early stage. The money needed at this point will depend to some extent on what is being performed – does it involve buying copies of published material, duplicating scripts, copyright fees, royalties to the Performing Right Society, or hiring copies? You may also need construction material for scenery, costumes and props.

There will be further expenses incurred during the next few weeks which will be dealt with later.

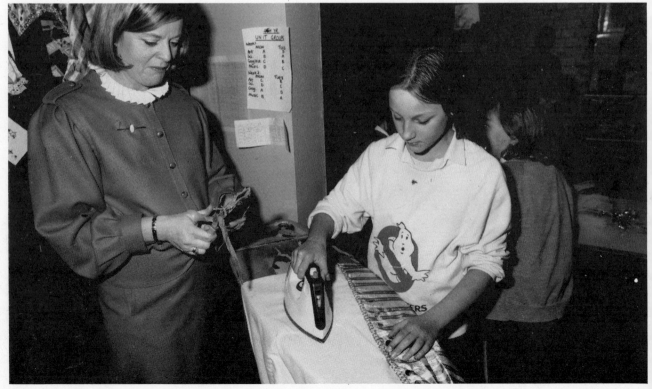

Make sure children are properly supervised if they are using or moving potentially dangerous equipment.

Don't forget to tell the ancillary staff about the project – you may need their help later on.

Spread the news!

You have now chosen the material to perform and all the staff have been informed.

Who else should be informed at this stage?

● Ancillary staff: caretaker (give him/her the performance date(s) if it's out of school hours or if you are planning weekend rehearsals), cleaners (they need to know which rooms/areas are being used for rehearsals after school), cook/catering staff (who may offer refreshment facilities and equipment), dinner-time supervisors (especially if dinner-time rehearsals are scheduled).

● Peripatetic teachers: especially if you want their help, or if the production includes children performing a piece of music taught by a peripatetic teacher.

● Friends of the school: those you may ask to help out in some way with the project. They, like you, are very busy people and need to be contacted in good time, especially if your performance is at

Christmas when people are generally busier than ever.

● Local authority officers and advisers: if you intend to invite local authority staff, then the sooner you can inform them of the performance dates, the better. Their 'free time' can quickly become fully booked, and an invitation can be sent much nearer the date, as long as they have been informed in good time.

● Parents: perhaps at the beginning of term, send a newsletter or information sheet to parents, including rehearsal and performance dates. Assuming the newsletter reaches the parents, you may receive offers of help. Make a list of those offers, acknowledge them and explain that you'll contact them at the appropriate time.

● Children: you are seeking a highly positive reaction from the children, so decisions about when, where and how they are told about the forthcoming performance needs thought and planning. To have the children buzzing with anticipation and enthusiasm will create a tremendous start to the project.

Speak now!

As a cautionary note, if you as director are not entirely happy with the choice of material, then say so *now*, because if you are responsible for the performance, a success will belong to everyone, but a failure will be *yours*, and yours alone! Time spent looking for a better alternative will be beneficial in the long run.

Now you can get down to the practical aspect of the project and begin to work with the children. Their involvement and development must be your main concern, for how you approach and work with the children, like all teaching, will set the standards for the whole project.

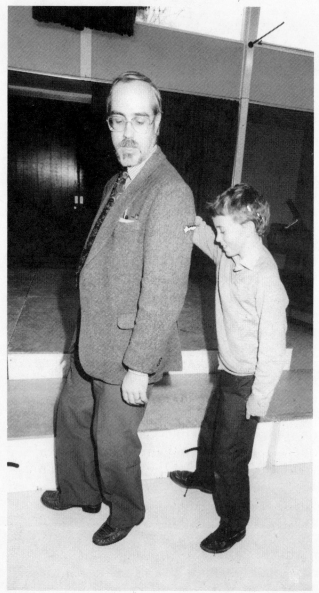

From now on you will be working with the children.

Checklist

● Will the performance be a play or a musical?

Play
    written especially for children
    adapted from a book
    Shakespearian
    mummers
    puppet
    revue/variety show
    write your own

Musical
    existing show
    cantata
    operetta
    masque
    old-time music hall
    pantomime
    write your own

● Will the material be
    already published in some form,
    a folktale requiring some rewriting, or
    original, with no copyright restrictions?
● Who is making the decisions?
● What age of child is involved?
● What resources/facilities are available?
● Are you directing it? If not, who is, and what is your role?
● What kind of audience are you aiming at?
● What is the financial situation?
● Do you need to start fund-raising activities?
● Have you informed
    the staff,
    ancillary staff,
    peripatetic staff,
    friends of the school,
    LEA officers and advisers,
    parents, and
    children?
● Have you allocated people to jobs?

Getting started

INTRODUCTION

Having made the major decisions outlined in the previous chapter, you should now be eager to begin the journey towards that final performance in a few weeks' time.

Keep in mind throughout that all the 'travellers' will be learning and developing, and that the journey should not be merely a means to an end. The next few weeks are a vitally important part of the whole project and require careful planning.

Just before you get started, have a look back through the Introduction to remind yourself of the benefits that you are aiming for during the project.

What needs to be done next, and where do you begin?

The script

Getting to know the script

You will first of all need to be familiar with the script and/or musical content of the project. At least two readings are suggested, unless of course you are the author, co-author, composer or major contributor, in which case the project may well be familiar enough!

Distributing scripts

If you are intending to obtain a number of scripts for distribution, number each one and write down the name of each person who has received one, with the script number alongside.

This is necessary for a number of reasons:

● If the scripts are borrowed/hired they will need to be returned, probably under your name, and someone (you?) will be billed for replacement costs.

● If the script is original, you may consider sending it to a publisher for possible future publication (depending upon how the performance goes!) and it is essential that the copyright owner is in possession of all printed copies.

● It will hopefully encourage everyone to take good care of their script.

Your most valued possession

If you will be using a printed script yourself, take it apart and paste each page into a loose-leaf folder or a stiff-covered, large exercise book, putting a blank page opposite each printed page, to be used for notes and markings during rehearsals. Leave a few blank pages at the beginning and end for notes and jobs when they come to mind, information on scene developments, general stage arrangements, and your cast list.

This folder or book will be your most valued possession, so you may feel a need to make a second copy to be locked away in the school safe. If you are fortunate enough to be working with a co-producer, a second copy is essential.

The script for *Jackie and the BEANSTALK Game* appears at the end of this book and may be photocopied.

The planning meeting

Before the meeting

It is helpful to have your own ideas about the development of the project but be prepared to make this a discussion point at your planning meeting. Colleagues will often feel a greater sense of involvement and purpose if some of their ideas are incorporated into the final performance.

It will be helpful to visualise each scene by sketches. Draw up ground plans which show the set and props from above each scene or scene change. If this can be done to scale, so much the better.

What else should you be looking for in the script? You will probably consider:
● technical problems which may arise in the staging,
● costumes,
● scenery,
● lighting,
● effects,
● entrances and exits.

Before the planning meeting you need to be very familiar with the script, the scene order, the characters and their development, the general development of the plot, and a

considerable amount of dialogue.

When you get to rehearsal you need to watch what is happening rather than just listening. The children will need support and encouragement in their efforts, particularly in the early days, and this should be given by you in facial and eye movements as well as vocally. You cannot do this with any credibility if you are desperately trying to follow the script in a book! The children deserve a well prepared producer just as your class deserves a well prepared teacher.

Once you feel confident about the script, to the extent that you could answer colleagues' initial questions, then arrange a planning meeting.

The agenda

1 Performance details
2 Jobs – staging
      – costumes
      – scenery
      – lighting
      – effects
      – props
      – music

– catering
– administration
3 Auditions
4 Rehearsal schedule
5 Any other urgent business
6 Dates of further meetings.

Ask the head to chair the meeting, since his/her involvement at this stage is crucial, and by chairing the meeting, approval of the project and the supportive aspect of his/her role will be established.

Performance details

It is necessary to remind colleagues of the basic details of the project and your concept of how the performance will materialise. It might also be helpful to create a little pressure and some panic by stating the time remaining before the performance date!

Jobs

First of all, check that everyone is happy about their area of responsibility. Also consider whether the project could have an influence across the curriculum. Discuss the possibilities so that the project can be seen in tangible, educational terms, and not merely as a one-off production with little relevance to what is going on in school.

The 'making' jobs are all dealt with in Chapter 3.

Auditions

Are auditions necessary?

The answer to this question will depend on the circumstances within your school and the age range of the children who will be involved. Some children may feel a sense of unfairness if certain children are 'picked by teacher'. At least if auditions are organised and take place, all the children who are interested in a solo part will have an equal chance.

First tell the children

Before you can begin to hold auditions, there must be children willing to take on a part. You need to 'sell' the idea of the performance to the children.

Gather them together and tell them about the type of performance, the plot in general terms, the main characters, the setting, the songs, some of the action, the performance dates, the amount of preparation time, the commitment needed and the enjoyment it can bring, the timetable for the next few days and what to do about auditions. Finally, stress that there is a part for everyone.

It is also important at this early stage to put across the idea of a whole school project, a co-operative effort.

Ask the children whether there are any urgent or important questions, then finish the meeting. No retreating now!

Having prepared your project notice-board, pin up the audition sheets as soon as possible and announce a closing date – a 24-hour time limit is often quite sufficient.

The audition schedule

Be prepared to give up one week for auditions. Lunch-times and/or after school will be the likely audition times. Often, a child's commitment to the project can be gauged to some degree by their willingness to give of their own time.

Give staff and children adequate notice of the audition details, and check that the venue is available and reasonably free from excess noise and disturbances. If your hall doubles as a dining room, avoid lunch-time auditions and rehearsals. An accompaniment from the depths of the kitchen, as crockery, cutlery, pots and pans are washed, stacked, dropped and eventually put away, can be quite distracting for young children.

Your schedule will be geared to your casting needs and more time will probably be required for the main roles, so start with these.

Preparing the children

Some children will have volunteered for more than one part, and there will probably be a compulsive auditionee who signs up for every part, including the front and back legs of the pantomime horse! You may decide to restrict the children's choice to, say, just two characters.

If possible, give the part of the script that has been chosen for audition to each child in sufficient time for them to become familiar with it.

Again, this creates a sense of the

RAYMOND IRONS

Build up enthusiasm by telling the children about the plot and characters, and singing some of the songs.

If children give up free time to audition, they are likely to do the same for rehearsals.

importance of the project and the commitment it requires. It also gives some children, who have signed up merely from peer group pressure, the opportunity to decide whether a main part is really what they want. You will find that children will soon let you know if they don't wish to audition, having seen the script.

Also, if the audition piece is a reasonably short scene, children are quite capable of learning their lines overnight and will come to the rehearsal with more confidence. This is of great help in discovering which children can cope with learning lines, and also means that at least a part of the script will have been learned before the first rehearsal.

Audition criteria

Naturally, you will want the most suitable children for the main parts, so before auditions begin, jot down the qualities that you are looking for in this particular project:
- strong, clear voice,
- projects the character,
- relaxed and uninhibited, moves easily,
- sensitive to those around, aware of the group effort,
- confident and competent reader,

- singing ability,
- enthusiastic and committed to the project,
- will benefit from being in a 'starring' role,
- ability to learn the script,
- initiative, ability to listen and learn quickly.

You may decide to draw up a matrix and put a score by each child as they audition.

AUDITIONS JACKIE AND THE BEANSTALK GAME CHARACTER: JACKIE*									
CRITERIA									
NAME	1	2	3	4	5	6	7	8	COMMENTS
Sally									
Katrina									
Donna									
Claire									
Catherine									
Hazel									
Sarah									
Gurjit									

The audition matrix used for the part of Jackie.

How much emphasis you place on each quality, and how formal you make the auditions, will depend upon you and the type of performance you are planning. Most of these qualities, however, are essential to any performance.

Organising the auditions

Try to organise the auditions so that a number of characters are involved, rather than hearing just one child at a time. This will help the individual child to feel less conspicuous and more a part of the scene, and you can also see which children blend well together – an important factor in your final casting.

I have found that the formality of the occasion brings out a number of positive points:
• The children can see that everyone is given a fair chance.
• It emphasises that the project is 'for real', and needs effort and commitment.
• It introduces the children to an essential part of theatre.

Talk to the children before beginning the auditions, explaining the criteria you have decided upon.

You may wish to begin your auditions with warm-up exercises, so that bodies and minds are more relaxed. Such exercises are often helpful before rehearsals and the performance.

If you have chosen to write your own material with just scene headings or a general plot, auditioning will perhaps be

less formal, and you can swap children into characters before final casting.

If you are staging a musical, choose a song or assembly hymn with which all the children are familiar and, in groups of about ten, ask them to sing in unison, but unaccompanied. You are then free to wander between and around the children and they are more likely to sing louder and in tune.

Casting

When you are close to the final casting, have a word with the class teachers to check the suitability of each child in taking on a major role.

It might be helpful to make a short list, say, two children per character, and give them a longer piece of script to look through, so that they can develop a little of the character. Move the children around during the final audition until you and your colleagues are satisfied that you have the best combination.

Let all your colleagues have a list of the final choices and then make an early appointment with the costume person for all your main characters.

Understudies

Think seriously about understudies at this point. If you have short-listed for the final auditions, ask the child who wasn't chosen if he/she would be an understudy. An understudy is often as word-perfect as the main character, and will enthusiastically step in if the main character drops out.

Type-casting

Type-casting should be avoided in certain cases. For example, it seems less than tactful to type-cast a well built, plump girl as the fat lady, for this merely exposes an aspect of her appearance she may not be particularly happy about. Instead, pad out a normal-sized child, who will be able to play the part without any unnecessary self-consciousness, so the audience can laugh without feeling embarrassed for the child. It may give the normal-sized child an insight into the problems of being fat, and they may even develop a better understanding of the problem.

In drawing up the lists be careful not to type-cast.

The chorus or crowd

Having decided on the main characters, you need to cast the other roles and make lists of children who will be in the chorus and/or the crowd.

Try to organise the chorus and crowd into pairs or small groups; this will help during rehearsals when asking the crowd to react to a piece of dialogue, and children will find it easier to practise outside rehearsal times in pairs or groups, rather than individually. It will also help in bringing everyone on stage in the finale, and in promoting a co-operative approach.

Two casts

If you have too many children wishing to be involved in the project have you considered two casts? This, of course, means two performances and two dress rehearsals but isn't as awkward to organise as it may seem initially.

Organisation is easier if the main characters remain the same for each performance.

Costumes for two casts are straightforward; simply arrange for similar-sized pairs of children to share.

Listen to each child as they sing in a group.

Check, of course, that all children from the same family are performing on the same night.

When you have completed the auditions and are happy with the cast list, your next task is to organise the rehearsal schedule.

If you have two casts, make sure the children's sizes correspond so that costumes can be shared.

Rehearsal schedule

Once you have fixed the date of your performance, work back from that date to organise rehearsals. Slot the dress rehearsal in on the morning of the performance day; for an evening performance, this will give you the afternoon to make any slight adjustments.

How much rehearsal time?

By the time you draw up the rehearsal schedule you should know quite accurately the amount of time necessary to make the project successful. This will be largely governed by the material you have chosen. If there is a lot of dialogue and interaction between a few main characters then this will take time to rehearse, largely during lunch-times or after school. If it is to be a musical show, then there is more scope for learning and rehearsing the songs in classroom time.

The need for commitment

Check that the main characters are available for the majority of the rehearsal times. If there is a clash of activities, emphasise the need for commitment and priorities.

I have always found the leaders of activities such as Girl Guides, Boy Scouts etc, to be most co-operative – when they are informed.

Include costume parades in the rehearsal schedule.

So if children feel that their loyalties are being divided and are unsure of how to cope with it, point out that their leaders would be quite willing for them to miss one meeting under these circumstances, and that the opportunity to take part in a school production happens maybe only once a year. If you leave the child to decide which has more priority, they may not choose your performance!

Talk with colleagues about your rehearsal schedule and how it fits in with their extra-curricular activities. It may be necessary and diplomatic to accede to other demands in the early stages, but a firm line must be taken as the performance day approaches. You cannot expect a successful conclusion to your project if it is under-rehearsed because the main characters were involved elsewhere at key rehearsal times. The head's support is vital!

A useful checklist

Set the performance date(s) and time.
Set the dress rehearsal date(s) and time (quite close to the actual performance).
Set weekend rehearsals if friends of the school or parents are involved in the performance, although too many weekend rehearsals can become unpopular with parents, and rightly so.
Set targets for the end of each rehearsal week.
Break down each week into rehearsal times: ie timetable, before school, break-time, lunch-time, after school.
Monday to Thursday gives adequate time for all aspects of your target.
Leave Friday free for working on an aspect that needs a lot of rehearsing, or for a run-through of the week's target.
Set specific dates for:
● a costume parade – set two or three of these to see how the costumes are progressing and what aspects need more time,
● lighting – children need to get used to the difference that lights make,
● scenery – this can make a significant difference to acting space as well as movement, so if scenery is not available, put a table or chairs or some other object in its place,

● props – these can create problems when they are are first used, so the sooner they are available the better.

Practising in groups

Choose whether to concentrate on small groups in the early stages, bringing larger groups together at a later stage, or to suggest teaching all the songs first to the massed chorus, breaking down the scenes later into smaller groups.

If your colleagues have offered to take some children for rehearsal, this is the opportunity for smaller, concentrated groups. For rehearsals in which you are not directly involved, discuss with your colleague how you envisage that particular scene or song. This can save time and embarrassment later when you find a scene has been rehearsed in an entirely different way.

Build up to a full dress rehearsal with props.

43

Pacing rehearsals

Start quite slowly, give praise and encouragement, and don't expect a polished performance by the end of the second rehearsal! This type of school project could be an entirely new experience for many children and they will need much explanation and support in the early stages.

Gradually, you will be able to quicken the pace and ask more and more of your cast. If the early stages have been positive and well founded, the children will respond enthusiastically to a quickening of pace.

Be very aware of pacing your rehearsals so that the children don't peak too early (or too late, of course!). This can create an anticlimax, the 'edge' vanishes and the children are left waiting and bored. Timing of the dress rehearsal is crucial. Make it as near to the performance as possible with just a short time in school for minor adjustments before the first performance.

Only bring together all the different aspects of the performance – costume, scenery, props, lighting etc – at the dress rehearsal.

Have an overall weekly target as well as an individual rehearsal target, so that you and your colleagues arrive at rehearsals with a clear idea of what you are hoping to achieve.

Keep everyone informed

The rehearsal schedule should be distributed to all members of staff, and posted in strategic places around school.

The children will need a schedule which gives the information relevant to them in clear, straightforward terms. If rehearsals are scheduled for after school or at a weekend, then parents need to be aware of this in writing and their permission needs to be sought. Give children and parents at least 24 hours' notice of after-school rehearsals, and ensure that the children are collected by their families, so the responsibility of their child has been

Warn parents in advance about after-school rehearsals and make sure all the children are collected.

handed over properly. Always give parents a time by which to collect their children and keep to this time.

You may decide to arrange a rehearsal space on your project-board and post up the rehearsal notices on a daily basis. It is always wise to send this note to each class before putting it on the project-board – not every child (or teacher) reads notice-boards!

Having organised all this you will probably find that the 'leading lady' goes home by bus and can't make after-school rehearsals, that the March Hare has simply not informed his parents that he is involved in the school project, and that even the weekly frisking session by parents failed to uncover any of your notes and letters to them. Parents first know of the project when they ring during the first after-school rehearsal to find out why their son is late home!

Rehearsing

Warm-up

Depending upon the time available at rehearsals and the children involved, you may start with some warm-up exercises to get the children in the right frame of mind and to loosen up their bodies. Explain to the children why the exercises are important, and join in with the children so that they don't feel you're making them do something that looks silly and causes embarrassment.

These exercises will also help audibility, as nerves affect voice projection and pitch.

A short routine can also be very useful just before the performance, in order to focus minds, temper nerves and create that corporate spirit and sense of team effort.

Learning lines

Learning lines can occasionally create a problem, but if your script is designed to involve quite a lot of speaking parts, then each child will not have too many words to learn.

Following the initial casting, give the main characters a copy of the script (remember to number each copy and keep a list of who's got which), asking them to look through it and highlight their part. It is often good practice to have a reading session, where the main characters sit with you and read through the script. Problem areas are likely to be highlighted during this session and you will also have the opportunity to explain the plot and make-up of the different characters in more detail.

Targetting

Once these children are happy about their lines you can begin to target them, so they become familiar with their part and how the characters fit in during the early stages, whilst later on you can target sections from memory. This targetting will need to 'dovetail' with your rehearsal schedule.

You will find with many children that the motivation of being chosen will spur them on to learning lines well in advance of their targets. I particularly remember one girl who had a duet to sing with a boy. During one lunch-time, I went through the song with them, and they quickly picked up their parts. By break in the afternoon, less than two hours later, the girl had learned the tune, words and harmony off by heart and proceeded to sing it to me on the playground, making a most pleasant change to my more normal playground duty activities of dodging footballs and the occasional low-flying child.

Key-wording

Lines become familiar as they are spoken and used, and so the more the children rehearse together, the more meaningful the words become, and the better they are learned. Never chastise children for forgetting lines, for they may develop a reluctance to use them and build up unnecessary anxiety, which only compounds the problem.

Often, a key word from you is enough to get them going again, whilst sometimes their fellow actors help out.

Key-wording is also a useful technique in teaching songs. After a couple of run-throughs, encourage the children to commit the words to memory and help them with key words – probably the first word of a line. Use an overhead projector so that the children are all focusing on the same area, holding their heads up well and taking in the visual image on the screen. Switch off when you think that the children have had time to memorise the words.

An advantage of memorising words early is that you can begin to develop movement and action at an early stage, giving children as much time as possible to become comfortable, relaxed and natural.

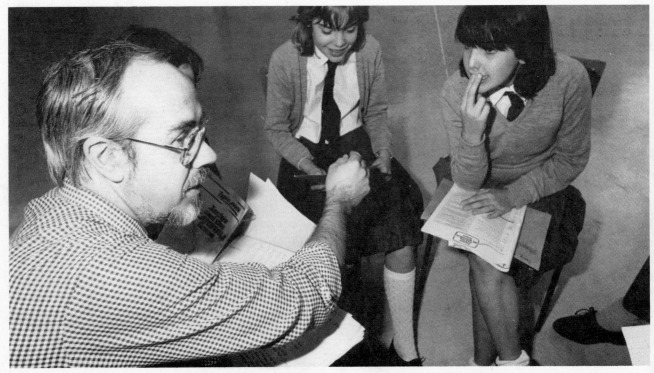

Hold a reading session with the main characters to help them become familiar with their parts.

To practise songs display the score using an overhead projector (remember copyright restrictions).

Recording lines and songs

If a child is having problems learning his or her lines, try recording them on a cassette or, better still, record the child reading their part. He or she can then take the cassette home to practise their lines, or simply listen to them over and over again.

This technique can also be applied to songs. Go through the song first with the child, pointing out rhythms and entries, and then give him a cassette of the song, melody and bass line, together with the music score so that he can see the little black dots in operation. This brings the child into contact with traditional musical notation.

Coaching and training

Before rehearsals begin, work out movements and mark them into your master copy, but also be prepared to amend these once the children start to bring movements to life.

Always be early for rehearsals and prepared to begin at the advertised time. Firstly, there is no time to waste, and secondly, punctuality by the producer sets a good example to the children. Thirdly, you are there to meet the children and can immediately set the tone for the rehearsal.

If some preliminary rehearsals have already taken place with the main characters and/or the larger groups, make a start with Act 1, Scene 1. This will be the audience's first glimpse of the performance and it needs to have an impact – a strong opening number, a mysterious sound, a lively overture, a thought-provoking opening line, complete darkness, a drum roll – some device which immediately catches the interest of the audience.

As you go through rehearsals take up different positions in the room so that you can get a visual and aural impression. Looking at the stage from various angles gives you a different appreciation of the production and may well highlight blind spots.

What do you hope to achieve by the end of each rehearsal? They generally give you and the actors time to prepare the script, songs and effects to a standard that is good enough to perform before an audience.

You will need to think about coaching, training and helping the children in a number of important areas:
● role-play,
● voice and role projection,
● moving naturally and using planned movements.

Work out movements before the rehearsal but be prepared to incorporate the children's ideas too.

Role-play

In order to be effective and convincing in any role you must first believe in it yourself. Any doubts will become quickly apparent to the audience, thus spoiling the illusion.

Getting into the character

It is important for you to discuss the roles of the main characters in depth and those of the other members of the cast in more general terms. Let the children suggest the type of person they think they are playing, having read the script.

Try to work with the children in getting 'under the skin' of characters. What kind of person are they? What interests them? What bores them? What were they like as children? What makes them laugh? What makes them sad? What role do they play in the main plot? Are they an extrovert or an introvert?

Also discuss each scene with the children and talk about how the characters react within it, what personality they take on and their role in the overall plot at that particular stage.

Expressing feelings

Feelings should be discussed, too. What feelings are the characters trying to portray and how can the children show these feelings? Young children, for example, may show sadness by bursting into a very loud crying bout, often uttering 'boo-hoo' in a piercing shriek! This is fine for pantomime, but of little use if the sadness is subtle, or there to evoke a sad response from the audience!

Expressing emotions in role-play is particularly difficult for young children, but

Children may find it difficult to portray feelings.

discussing the scene and even analysing the lines that develop an emotion will help them. If you have chosen material that contains emotions and feelings as important aspects, then you will need to tackle them, and not fight shy.

Other characteristics, such as deception, irony, sarcasm, teasing, gullibility, humour etc, need to be discussed, so that your main characters are aware of what their acting role is attempting to portray.

Avoid the temptation to shout from the back of the hall, 'You're supposed to be angry, Jonathan!', as poor Jonathan wrestles with his words at the first rehearsal. Both you and Jonathan need a better background to the material before rehearsals start!

Remember, too, that some, perhaps many, of the more serious, profound emotions are not within the experience of primary school children, although there will be some who, unfortunately, have experienced deep sadness or extreme fear.

Your knowledge of the children will guide you as to whether some of them would be subjected to reliving traumas in portraying these emotions. Certainly, your chosen material should not be heavy with such emotions; your project is not the place for extensive scenes of sadness or fear but more the vehicle for introducing the thrills, excitement and fun of live theatre to the children.

Voice and role projection

The voice and how it is used is a major aspect of the project which you will need to concentrate on, assuming your performance is not entirely mime or dance! Much of the communication between the children and the audience will be vocal, and an audience craning their necks or cupping their hands over their ears are sure signs that the words are dying.

So, the first aim is to achieve audibility

Children need to practise voice projection without shouting, breath control and articulation.

– being heard clearly by gran sitting in the corner at the back next to a noisy heater, but not sounding like a parade-ground sergeant major to people on the front row.

Articulation

Explain how to articulate words:
- first letter/syllable attack,
- certain syllable stress,
- clear endings, almost exaggerated,
- lilting, rhythmic voice,
- mouth shape,
- facial expression,
- differences in stress and dynamics,
- pitch of vocal sounds,
- aiming for key words in a sentence or paragraph.

Rushing lines

You may well find that children rush their words. Ask the children to say their lines as slowly as possible, so that they sound quite silly. Children enjoy doing this, and you can ask them to speed up gradually until you judge the speed to be correct. It is an aspect you will need to work at quite regularly, probably with the majority of children.

Natural pauses

You could also try movements between sentences so that there's a pause in the dialogue, but avoid dialogue whilst children are moving or have their backs to the audience. The audience doesn't really stand a chance of hearing the words clearly in these circumstances.

No shouting!

Also avoid asking children to shout. It can be irritating for the audience if the general dynamic is constantly loud. I usually ask the children to 'SOC it to us loud and clear!'
speak   Slowly
speak   Out
speak   Clearly

Directing the words

Suggest to the children that they direct their words over the audience's heads, into the corners, at certain people or objects, varying the direction so that all the audience not only hears but also feels included in the performance.

Don't ask children to aim their words at just one object. There will always be one child who speaks or sings the entire performance to the temperature control box in the far corner of the hall.

Avoid rushing lines and movement while speaking.

Breath control

Time spent on breath control exercises is most useful.

Check where children are taking breaths. They, like most people untrained in the skills of acting, will breathe when their body tells them to. But a naturally taken breath does not always convey the sense of a line, speech or song. Punctuation awareness will help, as will occasional pauses which create good effects.

Audibility will fade and probably disappear if a child runs out of breath or dries up, and line and word endings may tail off. You need to listen carefully, then quietly explain to an individual child or small group that their words are not clear. Practise lines with them, not in a large rehearsal, but at another opportunity in a quiet place.

Being aware of the audience

During rehearsals it is naturally difficult for children to be aware of an audience. Give them a specific area or object – maybe a chair or two, spaced around the hall – to which they occasionally address their lines. However, children may still turn away from the 'audience' as they continue to deliver

50

lines. Try to explain the problem to the children, and whilst doing so, turn and walk away! They will soon tell you that they cannot hear what you are saying. This is a useful discussion point to which you could add that you'd like to see all of their face when they deliver lines. This will need practice but that is what your rehearsals are for.

Mark stresses and pauses

It can be most helpful to read through the characters' lines with the child or a group of children and mark in the key words, stresses and pauses (you will already have done this on your copy), but not to excess because this will create confusion and do more harm than good. Reading through a scene with children will also help to highlight important points in the scene. The introduction of a new character, or an essential development in the plot, will need to be built up to so that each scene has a climax, giving the children something tangible to aim for.

Remember the audience as movements are planned.

Voice inflection

The inflection in the voice is something you will most probably have to work on with the children. Here you will need to explain and discuss the meaning that certain lines are trying to convey. Always try to achieve a natural tone in the voice, so that the child feels comfortable and the audience becomes aware and relaxed.

If time allows during rehearsals, swap your characters around so that different ways of saying the lines are heard, and children can begin to appreciate each other's problems of delivery.

Timing

Timing of lines, too, can be crucial, and often means the difference between a positive audience reaction and no reaction, especially in comedy. The children should work together on key lines, so that a rapport gradually evolves.

Again, without an audience, it is difficult for the children to judge audience reaction. Point out the moments in the performance when there will be some audience response.

Ask colleagues to sit in on some rehearsals and to react to the action. It is important to tell the children to pause whilst the audience reacts before continuing with dialogue. This is a high-order acting skill, needs considerable experience to judge well, and is often harder to achieve during the performance due to nerves. But the alternative is to lose a considerable amount of dialogue beneath audience laughter or comment. Ask a group of children to act as 'applause', as and when you indicate.

Songs

If your performance contains songs, then clarity of words is again essential. Stress good beginnings and endings and, in chorus work, the need to begin and end together – no straggly snakes on 's' sound-endings, no machine-gun effect on 'g' sound-beginnings. If you or a musical director are conducting or leading the singing from a position visible to the children, insist that they look at you. By mouthing the words, you will create a sense

51

All movement must be effective and not unnecessary or distracting for the audience.

of security in most, and, in a few under-prepared children, a sense of total reliance. For some movements, of course, looking at you will not be possible, so practice is necessary to achieve unity in sound production.

Moving naturally/planned movements

It is important when dealing with movement to remember that it is not the children, but the characters they are portraying who are moving. The credibility of the performance and the illusion you want to create for the audience must be based on characters, not actors.

If, for example, a ten-year-old is playing the role of a grandparent, you will need to discuss with the child how a 60- or 70-year-old grandparent moves. Not all grandparents are crippled with arthritis or have a hunchback and a walking stick! Observation of human movements, or even inviting grandparents to visit school and discuss this aspect, will help.

Basic movements

The aim of any movement on stage must be to add to the overall effect of the

performance. Unnecessary movements may distract or detract from the audience's enjoyment.

Basic movements to get characters on or off the stage, or from one area of the stage to another, are sometimes given in published material. Often, however, they give only very brief, basic guidelines and you will need to spend time in rehearsal working out movements.

Take it a scene at a time, and make plans of where props, scenery, exits and entries are, and how the characters can get to certain places. You may even cut out small cardboard characters and actually move them about on your plans!

Discuss and rehearse movements with the children, either on an individual basis or in groups during a crowd scene.

Crowd scenes

Crowd scenes and chorus movements will, of course, need more planning and more definite ideas prior to rehearsal. A crowd of 50 children cannot be expected to spend valuable rehearsal time improvising their own individual reactions and movements.

Work out movements for pairs, small groups or whole groups rather than individuals. The children in the crowd or chorus may not have wanted a main character role, and so feel much more at ease moving and reacting in a group.

For whole crowd/chorus movements, go for simple, effective visual moves that all the children can achieve with practice. Remember, you may have a wide age and ability range within these larger groups. If there is a mass swaying movement, make sure that they all start swaying the same way, perhaps towards a tangible object, such as a window, wall, picture or curtain. Left and right only cause confusion, and children end up looking at their feet to see which has R on it and which has L!

If drama is an integral part of the curriculum, then small group crowd scenes should be relatively straightforward to rehearse.

Discuss how different characters would move.

Body movements

Body movements (rather than moving the body) can be most effective and add greatly to the audience's perception of the performance. Children will tend to minimise body movements, as if they were being directed at a person standing next to them. Such movements will be lost to the vast majority of the audience and therefore would seem unnecessary.

Body movements need to be exaggerated, and you will need to judge the extent of exaggeration from different parts of the auditorium. Children will need practice at this skill, for at first it will seem awkward and unnatural to them. It is very similar to the projection of the voice – not too large (loud) as to 'knock over the front row', and not too small (quiet) as to be lost to those at the back.

Certain body movements hold certain associations for the audience. For example, striking, scratching or pointing to the head indicates memory, thought or realisation, whilst shrugging the shoulders means 'I couldn't care less' or 'I don't know'. Cupping the hand to the mouth will let the audience into a secret, whilst wagging the finger indicates a reprimand or 'you mark my words'. These are very useful movements, often reinforcing dialogue and, at times, replacing it.

When working out movements, make notes and sketches of what is finally decided upon, so that you have a record to refer to at the next rehearsal.

All the movements need to arise from the material and should 'move' the performance forward, whether they are done by individuals or the whole cast.

Masking and upstaging

As movements develop during rehearsals, watch carefully for masking or upstaging.

Masking is when one character comes between the audience and another character, hiding him from the audience. Upstaging is when a character has to turn his back on the audience in order to speak or be spoken to by another character. Both tend to detract from the audience's enjoyment and lessen the overall effect.

Final rehearsals

As the performance date approaches, you will need a number of rehearsals which concentrate on different aspects of the production.

Scenery and technical rehearsals

A scenery rehearsal is essential where strategies are worked out for moving scenery and the team of stage-hands (children, staff and/or parents) go through their paces.

A technical rehearsal for lights and lighting cues could be linked with a sound effects run-through.

Props, costumes and music

Props and costumes will also need to be rehearsed, but you may feel that the dress rehearsal is early enough as long as you have had a costume parade to check every costume and make notes of any problems.

If live music is part of your performance then a music rehearsal will be needed.

Run-throughs

Try to run through the complete

performance twice before the dress rehearsal, and make notes. During the first run-through it may be necessary to stop after each scene or where a break-down occurs and go over certain aspects. The second run-through might be allowed to run with discussion at the end.

Too many complete run-throughs will develop complacency and boredom, but too few will mean the performance is under-rehearsed, not just from the acting point of view but from many other aspects as well – scene changes, lights etc.

The dress rehearsal

The dress rehearsal should be eagerly anticipated with an air of quiet confidence and controlled nerves. If you can invite an audience, so much the better – perhaps the neighbourhood school, grandparents, people from the local old people's home, or parents with young children. An audience will give the performers a far greater sense of purpose and realism.

Remember that the dress rehearsal is not an occasion for stopping the performance to go over an under-rehearsed part, or even a known part that has not developed well. Leave time between the dress rehearsal and the performance to talk with the children who were involved in a problem area. But it is too late now to effect major changes. This would cause a considerable amount of insecurity and panic amongst the children.

The dress rehearsal should and surely must be held in school time. This, of course, can create organisational problems in providing cover for your class, so discuss arrangements with the head and/or deputy before in-school rehearsals. Flexibility, co-operation and goodwill are essential ingredients for this project; one of your most vital tasks is to maintain these qualities throughout the 'journey', in colleagues as well as yourself.

Stage management

Before the dress rehearsal, you will have allocated backstage jobs to all the necessary people. Have a list of these typed and prominently displayed, so that everyone backstage has a point of reference to check.

If you have a stage manager, then this will be his or her responsibility, and the two of you will need to discuss the dress rehearsal, both before and after.

Try to organise everything at the dress rehearsal as it will be in the performance, even the audience participation items, whether there is an audience or not. Use the rooms and areas backstage that will be used during the performance so that the children know where to report to.

Timing

If you are able to let the dress rehearsal run through to its conclusion, you will have a good idea of how long the performance will last. (Remember to add on a few extra minutes for the 12 encores demanded by the audience!)

Parents can then be informed of the approximate finishing time for collecting children, if for some reason they are not part of the audience. However, do stress that the timing can only be approximate.

During the dress rehearsal use the backstage areas which will be used for the performance.

Maintaining morale

When the dress rehearsal ends, gather all the children together and, whatever the outcome, praise the good parts and maintain (or try to raise) confidence and morale. It is too late for major changes, so accept that the dress rehearsal was the first proper run-through, and it really will be all right on the night.

However, do not be lulled into complacency, for there are aspects that can only improve with practice, such as scene changes and lighting synchronisation. No matter how uplifting the audience is, if these aspects are not properly prepared by the dress rehearsal, the odds are that the first performance will not see a great improvement. All the technical side of the production needs to be ready for the dress rehearsal.

The children performing are quite another matter. I never cease to be amazed at children's ability to rise to the occasion. It is quite staggering to watch a child give an inspired performance just a few hours after an ordinary, even lack-lustre dress rehearsal.

Again, however, if children don't know their lines by the dress rehearsal, no amount of rising to the occasion will change this.

The final rehearsal stages can become a testing time for your sanity, but you are the one person throughout the project who knows what's happening, is seen to be calm and smiling at all times, never shouts, and exudes complete optimism that 'it'll be fine on the night'.

By the way, whilst you've been tied up with rehearsals over the past few weeks, what's been happening backstage?

Have you kept an eye on costume, scenery, props? Is the painting on the scenery dry? Is there any scenery yet? Do you recollect ever seeing that team of costume helpers who promised to come into school last week?

Move on to the next chapter to see what's going on in the 'making' departments.

Try to organise everything for the dress rehearsal exactly as it will be during the performance.

BOB BRAY

Even if the dress rehearsal goes badly, try to raise morale and boost the children's confidence.

Checklist

Are you familiar with the material for your performance?

Have you arranged a planning meeting?

Are your colleagues happy about their responsibility areas?

Will auditions be held?

How will auditions be organised?

Have you decided upon the cast?

When will rehearsals take place?

Have you worked out the rehearsal schedule?

What are your aims for each rehearsal?

Have you organised the final week's rehearsals?

What was the dress rehearsal like?

Scenery, costume and props

Scenery, costume and props

INTRODUCTION

All aspects of the 'making' part of your project need to be started as early as possible. As long as items can be safely stored, the sooner everything is made the better. This will allow the children to become used to scenery and props and give them time to feel 'natural' on the stage when using them.

At the initial planning meeting, arrange regular (weekly) meetings with colleagues who are responsible for each area. If you have included a scenery run-through and costume parade in your rehearsal schedule, colleagues will have target days to aim for.

The three 'making' areas are:
- scenery,
- costume,
- props.

For each area your first considerations should be:
- Is it necessary?
- Is it possible?
- Will the items enhance the production?
- Will the audience understand and appreciate what has been made?

Finding the time

Making costs time and effort, which are not available in great quantities under the pressures of the school day. Unless the making can be incorporated into the project using timetable time, then much of it will have to take place out of normal school hours.

If you and your colleagues are not prepared for this intrusion on your own time, keep all the items as simple and quick to make as possible, and at an early date set a basic design, a straightforward pattern and an easy plan. By doing this, making the scenery, costume and props will not grow out of proportion to your main concern in putting on a performance – the children.

On the other hand, if the 'making' is accepted as an integral part of the project and the children are involved, it is quite acceptable to use timetable time. After all, maths, CDT, problem-solving, a great deal of focused discussion and many manipulative skills will be used. The finished items will be tangible results of the children's work, and they will be working for a purpose.

Involving parents

Before starting your project it is a good idea to discuss school policy on parental involvement with the headteacher.

Parents will often offer their services at times like this, and there are probably many more parents who only need to be asked. Have a clear idea of what extra help you need and how you are going to organise it. Parents, like teachers, are busy people and you need to be well organised early on.

By being involved in this way, parents, teachers and children will hopefully form a better understanding of each other and a

greater confidence in what the school is trying to do.

Keep it simple

Resist the temptation to design on too grand a scale, because problems can arise when you need to move scenery, or you find props are unmanageable for the children, or costumes simply look ridiculous.

Often the most effective results come from simple ideas.

No one aspect of your production should put the other aspects in its shadow, and costumes, scenery and props should simply add to the overall production. You are aiming for a balanced production of high standards all round.

Scenery

At an early date, arrange a meeting with the colleague who has agreed to oversee the scenery. Topics for discussion at this meeting will include:
● basic scenes, number and subject,
● construction ideas,
● special effects,
● materials to use,
● covering the scenery,
● backcloths,
● team of helpers.

How many scenes?

During your reading of the script, you will have noted the number of scenes and the scene changes required. Try to avoid too many scenes requiring a scene change. You won't have the time or the resources to construct more than two or three different scenes, and more than that would take an inappropriate amount of time in scene changing. This can impose upon the

61

continuity of the performance and spoil the audience's enjoyment.

It is interesting for the audience and the participants if you can devise a change of scene, perhaps an interior and exterior, realistic and escapist. You could start with a living-room scene, change to the street outside, or a far-off planet, or the giant's castle, and then return to the living room. This adds interest by giving a different visual effect, as well as a change of mood.

Having decided upon the number of scene changes, you will need to discuss the details of each scene.

Remember that the scenery needs to be bold enough for the person at the very back of the hall to take in at first glance what it is depicting, yet not too bold as to be overwhelming or distracting. Small detail will be virtually lost to them.

Make sketches of your ideas and experiment with different colour combinations so that you have a fairly good idea of the results before the construction begins.

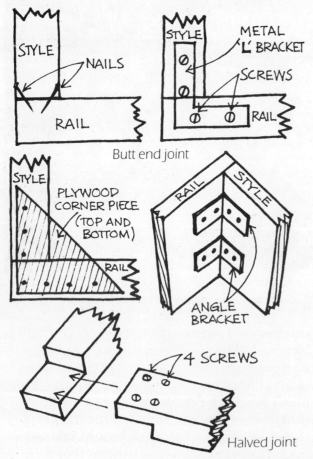

Butt end joint

Halved joint

How to make flats

You will need to consider the type of scenery construction that best suits your stage and resources.

Most scenery comprises small units which can be used in a number of ways, sometimes creating quite complex sets.

The main items of scenery in the theatre are flats – wooden frames (usually constructed from 7.5cm by 2.5cm wood) covered with tightly stretched canvas or hessian.

They vary in size, some as large as 5.5m by 2.5m, but if they are too large they cannot be easily moved or combined with other flats. If you intend children to move scenery, then size and weight must be an important factor in construction.

Aim to make the flats lightweight, adaptable and easy to handle and move.

The main joint system used in the frame construction is the mortise and tenon joint. The mortise (hole) is in the rail and the tenon is in the stile (vertical rail).

This means the base of the flat has just one surface – the bottom rail – making it easier to slide when being moved.

If mortise and tenon joints are too complex, then butt end or halved joints can be used. Finally, the whole frame is glued and secured at each corner with screws.

These frames can be used singly or lashed together, usually with lightweight rope, to give you the required length of scenery. They can also be hinged together to give you a free-standing screen effect.

The basic construction of a flat can also be used for doors and windows. Glass should not be used, although a leaded effect can be achieved with stretched black tape. Remind the children not to put their hands through the 'glass'!

Instead of covering the flat with canvas or hessian, you could use hardboard which would enable you to create two scenes on one flat, since both sides could be painted or papered.

Safety

An extremely important aspect of any scenery is safety. You must be 100 per cent sure that none of the scenery will fall. Flats need weights and braces, or in some cases buttresses, which can be either hinged (allowing for easier handling and storage), or screwed. Weights may well be found amongst your PE equipment, normally used to hold down posts which support nets for indoor games.

Be prepared for a fire inspection; the fire officer may insist that fireproof material is used, or that fireproofing is carried out.

Fireproofing can be done in school with a spray, or by making up your own solution. For heavyweight materials, use 425g boric acid and 285g sodium phosphate to 4.5 litres of warm water. For lightweight or more delicate materials, use 285g borax and 225g boric acid to 4.5 litres of warm water.

The materials requiring fireproofing need to be soaked or very liberally sprayed. If you are in any doubt about this, contact your local fire brigade who will gladly offer advice.

Cardboard box scenery

If you have neither the expertise nor the resources to construct flats, but can acquire a number of fairly stout cardboard boxes from local shops or firms, then you could build your own scenery from these.

Build up the boxes like building bricks so that you've got a fairly rigid but light structure. Masking tape, heavy duty adhesive tape or brown gummed paper will secure the boxes together.

Construct some sort of frame for hanging a door.

The structure can then be papered, or you could stick flat sheets of cardboard on to the boxes, giving a sound, flat surface to paint.

These blocks can be used for two different scenes, back and front, and can be rotated quite easily.

Cut out 'hand-holes' on each side of the block – a Stanley knife will do the job adequately – so that while moving it, one hand can steady it while the other slots into the hole.

Creating different effects

Of course, the tops of your blocks could take on different shapes by fixing sheets of stiff card in whatever shape you require. By missing every other box of the top row, you would achieve a crenellation effect suitable for a castle. Rooftops with chimneys can be built up and when painted or papered can look most effective.

For an interior scene, wallpaper gives a more than adequate effect and also helps to cover up joins in the boxes. If you are using two or more blocks, there will be slight gaps between them, These can be covered or disguised by hanging curtains, or a tree could be attached to the blocks for an outdoor scene.

Create doors and windows by leaving a certain number of boxes out of the overall construction.

A window can be open from the front and the back, or have a suitable 'view' painted on.

You will need a frame to hang the door on: 5cm by 2.5cm battens, glued to the boxes to form the architrave, is more than adequate to support a door.

If you are constructing a door, aim to make it as lightweight as possible. A wooden frame covered by a sheet of cardboard and then painted or papered can be most effective.

Fixing doors into flats can be slightly more complex as you will need to replace the bottom rail with a rounded iron sill. This avoids a rather ungainly entrance caused by tripping over the wooden rail!

You will need to find somewhere to

make and store sizeable pieces of scenery. Remember to protect floors.

If you decide to construct the scenery away from where the performance will take place, make sure you can transport it easily.

Using screens

Another simple idea is to use the school's medical screens, if you have them. Cover them with strong paper and paint the scene on. Two sets of screens joined together will give eight sections, so you have a scene for each side of the screens, while the outer sections can be folded in to give different effects.

A single background

You may decide that making scenery is not possible or necessary for your performance, and that a background scene will be enough. This can be achieved in a number of ways.

Perhaps one of the simplest yet effective ways is to cut out paper or thin card shapes, and staple or pin these to a back wall. A similar idea is to assemble a frieze; this can be prepared in class with the children and will be a most attractive and colourful addition to the performance.

One school chose the cut-out paper method for its nativity presentation, stapling 'hills' and 'flat-roofed houses' to the back wall and fixing 'palm trees' to the upright support posts of the PE apparatus. A star was suspended from a cross-beam of the apparatus, and the whole effect was quite magical.

Backcloths

Backcloths can also be effective as background scenery. You will need, of course, a considerable amount of material and either a wooden frame if the backcloth is static, or a means of rolling it up if you envisage more than one scene.

In either case, you will need to devise a method of hanging the backcloth; brackets attached quite high on the back wall are probably the simplest way. Remember to attach a weight to the base of the backcloth to stabilise it. This could be a batten or even a cardboard tube from a carpet shop, cut to the required length. It also helps in rolling and unrolling the backcloth.

Backcloths can also be made from large sheets of polythene available from builders' merchants. When sprayed rather than painted they can provide a most effective scene.

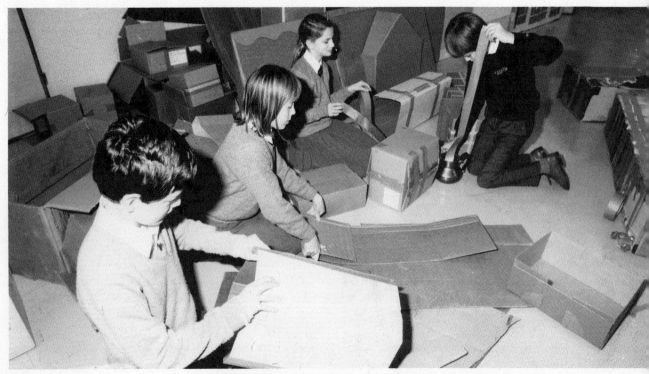

A pile of sturdy cardboard boxes and some brown gummed paper provide the raw material for scenery.

As the scenery begins to take shape, a space is left for a window and some of the boxes have been painted.

Painting the scenery

Before painting any of the scenery, experiment first with colour mixes and on small pieces of the material which forms the scenery, since paint will often dry to a different shade.

Consider the overall colour effect of the background scenery; if it is too pale, the performers' faces will tend to 'disappear', but if it is too bold and fussy it will distract the audience's attention.

If you have made flats with canvas, it is necessary to prime them with a base coat of paint and size (a type of glaze) mixed together. This helps the canvas to stretch out, and provides a base on which to paint the scene.

Alternative ideas

Pageants and revues will often require very little background scenery. However, the use of good quality slides and a projector will enhance the visual effect. Another effect which can be quite exciting is to synchronise a sound-track with the slides. This can all be recorded previously and, with the right equipment, will virtually run itself during the performance. An alternative is to produce the sound live,

which will involve more children in the performance.

Outdoor performances

So far the ideas concerning scenery have assumed that the project and final performance will take place in your own school.

Your initial discussion meeting about scenery will follow a different path if the performance is at another venue or outdoors. In either situation try to make do with as little scenery as possible, because

Paper shapes stuck to the back wall is a simple idea.

65

the problems of transporting it, erecting it or covering it during inclement weather are just some that will take up a good deal of time in planning. Also, scenery and effects that enhance the performance in your own familiar surroundings do not always have the same enhancing effect elsewhere.

You may also encounter the problem of where to hang your backcloth when performing outdoors!

You may well decide that costume and props become more important if your performance is to take place elsewhere. They are certainly more transportable than scenery.

Outdoors costume and props are more important.

Costume

The costumes are arguably the most important aspect of the whole performance.

You will have some basic costume ideas from having read the script, but a meeting with your colleague who has agreed to

oversee this aspect is needed at an early date. You may include the scenery person as well to discuss general colour schemes. (If colour schemes and matching costume colours to background colours are high on your list of priorities at an early stage, you are infinitely better organised than I have ever been!)

What is available?

It is always helpful to ascertain at a very early stage what is available in the way of costume and/or material at school – and how much of it can be used for the project. Make sure that you are not designing costumes that devour the rest of the year's stock!

Parents of present and ex-pupils and friends of the school will be only too glad to get rid of clothes that are no longer needed. We even had some delivered in suitcases and were told we could keep the lot – suitcases as well. So not only was our school wardrobe department expanded, but we also had storage facilities!

Storing costumes

Storage can be a problem at any time, but as costumes are completed they need a safe, relatively clean resting place.

There is usually one space within a school that can be acquired for storing costumes, even if it's just a washing line and coat-hangers! Dry cleaners will often let you have plastic covers for clothes, but a piece of material draped over will keep some of the dust away.

Where a large space or more than one space is available, why not invest in wardrobes? Let parents know you are on the look-out for wardrobes to store costumes – you may be quite surprised at the offers. Even if they cannot provide things themselves, parents will ask around and may know of somebody somewhere who is just about to get rid of a wardrobe. Do check, however, for signs of woodworm; the school maintenance department of the local authority are none too pleased when called upon to replace the school's window frames due to imported pests!

Costume specifications

Having decided that costume will enhance the overall effect, you need to consider two areas:

Curtains can be used for a number of costume ideas.

● main characters wearing specialised costumes,
● general costumes for crowds, the chorus, or a large group in the same costumes.

You will then need to decide upon the period setting for costumes eg Roman, medieval, Tudor, Victorian, present day, futuristic or possibly a combination of periods.

How closely are you going to recreate the costume of the day? A general idea is more helpful to the audience, since fine detail will be too small to be appreciated by all except the front row.

Once the cast list is known, make out a costume specification for each character and each group. Here is Jackie's specification from *Jackie and the BEANSTALK Game*.

CHARACTER	'ARTIST'	COSTUME REQUIREMENTS	SCHOOL	HOME	GOT
JACKIE	KATRINA	'HECTIC' BLOUSE/ SHIRT		✓	
		WELL-WORN JEANS		✓	
		TRAINERS		✓	
		BRACES		✓	

This was straightforward costuming which was available from home, although the 'chickens' in the same production required a little more thought and time.

CHARACTER	'ARTIST'	COSTUME REQUIREMENTS	SCHOOL	HOME	GOT
CHICKENS x16	VARIOUS IN 8 PAIRS	VEST — DYED	✓	✓	
		TIGHTS — DYED	✓	✓	
		'COMB'	✓		
		FEATHERS	✓		
		'BODY'	✓		

They spent a considerable amount of time making their own feathers and body, and became extremely proficient at preening!

Dressing a large number

If you are involving a large number of children wearing costumes of a similar style, aim for simplicity. The T-shaped top or tunic is easy to make and will be suitable for a number of periods in history. Period 'jewellery' and appropriate headgear will also help the audience to focus in on the right period.

With large groups, suggest costume that can be acquired readily from home with perhaps a small item to be worked on at school.

Guidelines for parents

If you are asking parents to help out with costume, give them good notice and quite accurate ideas of what is required. A 'costume sheet' with sketches and suggestions for material and how to make them up is most helpful to parents, and can avoid discrepancy between costumes due to some parents being less proficient than others. Costumes should unite, and the children should not be either over- or under-costumed. If *HMS Pinafore* was your choice, and you asked parents to make a sailor suit for their child, the results would be quite amazing and quite diverse, and in some cases non-existent! So set definite guidelines and have a costume parade just to check that they are developing along the right lines.

You may be able to organise a group of parents to work in school with children and teachers. In this way, explanations can be given when needed, and parents will gain a better insight into what goes on behind the scenes.

Simple ideas

Many schools organise T-shirts with school badges or names and we developed the idea to costume some of our productions. A logo or motif was designed, usually by the children, with amendments and adjustments to satisfy the printer.

As this was a non-profit making exercise, we were able to charge parents cost price.

Tunic and tights provide a simple base for costume.

68

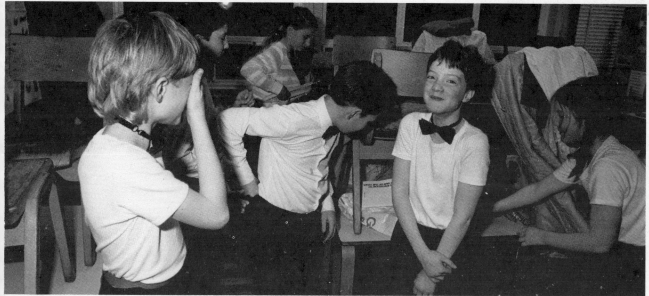

For a large number, keep costume simple, such as these black bow ties, white shirts and black trousers.

Instead of a professionally printed T-shirt you could print your own, assuming you have the facilities. Screen printing is a most satisfying experience for the children and printing their own logo or motif on the T-shirt they'll wear in the performance will have much more meaning for them.

The logo could also be printed on to paper for programme covers, frontispieces for the music stands, or invitations to attend the performance.

On another occasion we were undecided about how to costume the chorus until a 'fairy godfather' (a parent from a local firm) arrived with a box of very smart black bow ties, which were no longer needed by his firm. Our costume problem was solved – a chorus in black and white: black bow tie, white T-shirt or round necked shirt/blouse, black trousers/skirt/ski pants/leggings, white pumps/soft-soled shoes.

Not only did the children look good but they also enjoyed wearing the costumes. Just one or two were disappointed that the bow ties didn't rotate like propellers!

Throughout the year, remind parents that if they are throwing out old sheets, blankets, towels, dresses, material and so on, they might throw them towards the school. In this way you will gradually build up useful supplies which could save a last minute panic as you desperately try to costume 140 thieves for your version of 'Ali Baba'.

Choose the right materials

Remember that whatever material is used, the finished garment must be comfortable to wear. There is nothing worse for a performer of any age than to feel either uncomfortable or silly in what they are

Remember that fur fabric makes the wearer quite hot.

wearing. There can be no justification for making an uncomfortable or silly costume and insisting that a child wears it except, of course, where this is an integral part of the performance.

The material should not be itchy or prickly, and beware of some man-made materials, which will often 'hug' the wearer unless there is another garment underneath and which may look odd in a period production.

Particularly shiny material can be irritating to the audience, since it tends to flash and distract when light shines on it. However, if the character demands a loud, flashy costume, then a lurex-type creation will be just right.

Try to avoid very expensive material; you can be sure that if any costume is destined to have blackcurrant juice spilt on it or chewing gum stuck to it, it will be the most expensive one! Also, it is more than likely that an audience some distance away will not appreciate an expensive material.

Animal costumes

For animal costumes or 'skins', the fur fabric that looks most realistic becomes extremely hot to wear. Looseness is therefore preferable to a tight-fitting skin, and if you can build into the costumes an air conditioning system or refrigeration unit, it is very much appreciated by the occupants! It is important to have animal skins ready as soon as possible to give the wearers a reasonable time to practise and get used to them. Be especially careful about the positioning of the face, especially with regard to eye holes and the breathing hole.

Period costume

For a period production, you will find many suitable books which give a very good idea of both styles and colours. Odds and ends such as lace, belts, buttons, braids and costume jewellery will all help to give period costumes a more authentic look.

The right colour

Colour can be an important aspect of costume, since certain colours will indicate to the audience a character's personality. The 'baddie' is usually in black or a dark

costume, with the 'goodie' in white. Red often suggests a fiery or even a questionable character. Dorinda, the French damsel in distress from *Guy of Warwick*, looked just right in a vivid red 'designer' outfit with black, lacey trimmings, whilst Felice, the heroine, was in a white, pretty costume.

Getting used to costume

When your performance is 'in the round' or a similar setting, the costume will necessarily come under closer scrutiny and you will need to be a bit more careful. Although the audience, in the main, has come to see the children, and is unlikely to be too critical of costume, that isn't a licence to let the performance down with unfinished, unsuitable costume.

A suitable, appropriate and well made costume will, on the other hand, enable the performer to take on the role of that character in a more natural and convincing way.

You may find that some costumes give a

Some costumes will take a lot of getting used to!

Make sure that headgear fits well and won't cause disruption by falling off during a performance.

different feeling to everyday actions like walking, sitting and bending. Children may need time to get used to their slightly amended ways of moving. Period costumes, especially, will feel strange, and getting bulky costumes and crinolines through narrow openings in the scenery may cause problems.

Queen Elizabeth I's entry to welcome Sir Walter Raleigh home from America during a school musical production was far from majestic, for as the dress was wider than the entrance, she turned and came in sideways. Fortunately, that small problem was discovered in rehearsal with sufficient time to alter the entrance; the dress was too superb to alter.

Headgear and footwear

Headgear can create problems, too – mainly in keeping it on, but also in casting shadows over faces. As far as possible, provide individually measured headgear that fits well and won't fall off. If it does, children will more than likely pick up whatever has fallen and accentuate the mistake.

Footwear is the aspect of costume that the audience take least notice of, and to spend a great deal of time attempting to be authentic will not necessarily be time well spent. On the other hand, the effect of a beautifully costumed and presented nativity tends to be spoiled as Mary sits gently down in the hay only to reveal dirty pink trainers.

Cardboard buckles sewn into a loop of elastic and fitted over a shoe will give an authentic look covering quite a long period of history. Wellington boots with leather (or a substitute) folded over the top with a trim of lace look quite 'cavalierish'. Wellingtons sprayed silver look most effective for futuristic or science fiction performances.

For the giant in *Jackie and the BEANSTALK Game* we used lightweight wooden blocks taped securely to the soles of large Wellingtons, and covered the whole contraption with fur fabric. This made the giant more than 20cm taller, and needed a considerable amount of practice time.

Remember that pumps or soft-soled shoes will create less noise than ordinary shoes. This could be an important consideration if your stage comprises rostra blocks which amplify sound enormously.

Specialist costumes

Occasionally you may need to look beyond the school and parental resources for a specialist costume. Other schools, particularly secondary schools used to putting on productions, may be able to loan a certain costume.

Alternatively, contact your local theatre or amateur theatrical group. Be prepared to pay a loan fee or suggest a small donation.

On very rare occasions you may even consider hiring a costume from a reputable costumier. Hiring, of course, is not cheap, and you also run the risk of damage.

Budgeting for costume

Costume, like scenery, is an area of your project requiring funds almost from the outset. If you know your approximate costume budget at the beginning of your project then you will immediately have an idea of what can be done and also what is beyond the budget means.

The giant wore built-up wellingtons covered in fur.

Remind your colleagues from the beginning to get receipts of all expenditure so that proper accounts can be kept, and monies spent out can be properly reimbursed.

Props

Properties, or props as they are more often called, are all those items other than scenery which the audience sees as the curtain rises and those which are brought on during the performance.

Like scenery and costume, props help to create the illusion for the audience, and add visual reinforcement to the words and actions.

Deciding on props

Props fall into two categories:
• personal – those that are carried by the performers, such as a magnifying glass,

paper, a fairy's wand, a walking stick etc;
● stage – those that are part of a scene, such as furniture, curtains, ornaments and pictures, or those that will be brought on during a scene.

Go for simple props which are easy to acquire or make, and will convey their message quickly and totally to the audience. Props which leave an audience wondering why they appeared will begin to destroy the illusion you have created.

Some published scripts will include a suggested list of props, but it is worth while to go through the script and make your own list as well.

Be prepared to add to your list as you see the production developing in rehearsal. Children will often suggest props to highlight actions and words, and you may incorporate some of their ideas.

Try to organise the main props in good time; last-minute prop making can be quite stressful and the results aren't always successful.

Store props carefully, as it is annoying to find, on dress rehearsal day, that a prop made five weeks previously looks as if it's spent a week at the local playgroup.

Where to find props

When you have made your list, write alongside each item how it is going to be acquired:
● colleagues – teaching and non-teaching,
● children – list your requirements on a newsletter or the costume sheet,
● friends and local firms – offer a mention in the programme.

If the props are still proving difficult to find you will need to make or hire them.

You will probably find that the children are most keen and very efficient in collecting props. This can greatly lessen the burden on you (or the delegated colleague) and save a considerable amount of time, but make sure you see these props well before the dress rehearsal, in case they have misunderstood what you were asking for.

Avoid hiring props or borrowing valuable or sentimental items. You will be constantly worrying about damage or loss, and I would suggest you do not become involved in insuring items.

Children may be able to make their own props.

Making props

Making at least some of your props will be almost inevitable.

Who is going to make them? If no-one has volunteered to oversee the props, break down your list and ask if Cheryl could make the golden egg or Barry the fairy's wand complete with flashing light. This helps to spread the work and colleagues may be far more willing to make a single item than face the prospect of making all of them.

Give accurate details of the item you require, what its purpose is, and who is going to be carrying it if it's a personal prop.

As colleagues take on this task, explain that any expense will be reimbursed and remember to ask for receipts.

Finding materials

You will need to have a good look round school for suitable materials. The following are often useful:
cardboard boxes
cardboard (various
    thicknesses)
paper
papier mâché
material

73

feathers
wood-battens
sheets
glue
Lego, Meccano etc
wire
cane (soak it first)
polystyrene
packing materials
sticky tape
Sellotape

If accuracy is important, browse around the library for books with illustrations of the articles you need to make.

If you are contemplating breaking vases, or irreplaceable ornaments, break one first and glue it lightly back together. 'Untouched' breakables have a nasty habit of bouncing which causes panic in the performers and amusement in the audience.

For props which are not intended for disposal or destruction, but are made from disposable material (shopping-lists, paper flowers, letters etc), make a spare one just in case.

When using mirrors or pictures for wall hangings, remember that they will reflect light and this can be most off-putting to an audience. If they are absolutely necessary, angle them away from a direct reflection to the audience. Sometimes a light covering of size solution, soap or Vaseline will help to dull the reflection. Check their weight, too, for although your scenery is magnificently made, it was not built to support a great deal of hanging weight. The positioning of picture hooks, screws or nails should be carefully considered.

Rehearsing with props

Props can be incorporated into rehearsals as they are completed, for the sooner the real props can be used the better. Should any prop still feel awkward or look out of place after a few rehearsals, reconsider its design and use. Awkward or unsightly props will become more and more awkward and unsightly as time goes on.

Before the props are available, use something that is a similar size, even if it's an old cardboard box or a metre rule, but don't introduce these until scripts are no longer needed, otherwise you will be asking a child to juggle with a script in one hand and a prop in the other.

Managing props

You will need a volunteer to get stage props into their correct positions at the right time. That person will need helpers, so this is a good opportunity for children to be involved. I have found our stage-hands to be extremely reliable and hard-working, very quickly memorising the order of props and scene changes.

Go for simple props which enhance the overall effect and don't distract the audience unnecessarily.

A metre rule replaces an unfinished prop in rehearsal.

Why not make their job part of the performance and name your stage-hands in the programme?

Stage props need to be as close to the set as possible without creating traffic jams backstage. If their position on stage needs to be accurate each time, put a mark on the floor so that the stage-hands know exactly where each prop goes. Scenery, too, should have positions marked with sticky tape.

A props table or box

When props come from the stage having fulfilled their role, replace them in the same storing positions. This way you know where things are for the next performance and people backstage get to know where obstacles are situated.

Place personal props on a table or tables, again quite close to the set, so that as performers gather backstage it is easy for them to collect their props before they go on.

If you cover the table with a light-coloured paper you can label areas for certain props, or even draw round their shape so that replacement is simple. However, the table as well as stage props need checking after each performance to make sure everything is there that should be there. Any valuable props should be looked after by you, and not left on general display.

An alternative to a table is a props box. This is particularly useful for gathering all the items together and for storage.

Keep a list backstage

When all the items are ready, go through the script with the colleague in charge of props during the performance, and make out a list of props and what happens to them scene by scene. Display a copy of the list backstage as a check for the stage-hands and for the performers.

After the final performance, check that all props have been returned. If props were made by the children at school or for particular characters, you may wish to give the props to the children.

Some props which you may feel would be useful for a future production will need storing carefully and safely.

Know what you want

Scenery, costume, and props will probably be the most expensive area of your project, and so they need to be right first time! Before starting to make anything, you need fairly definite ideas of what is required and how to achieve it.

These three aspects alone cannot make your performance successful, but they can add a tremendous amount to the audience's perception and appreciation of the performance.

Decide what you want, then how to achieve it.

Checklist

General

Is it necessary?
Is it possible?
Will it add to the audience's enjoyment?
Have you organised child and parent
    involvement in the making aspect?
What financial arrangements have you
    made?
Keep all receipts.

Scenery

Who is going to oversee this aspect?
Make a list of different scenes.
Are you performing indoors or outdoors?
How many changes are there?
How much scenery can you cope with?
Have you sketched your ideas in colour?
How are you going to construct the scenery?
What materials/equipment will you need?
What safety devices are you considering?
What about fireproofing?
Are you painting or wallpapering the
    scenery?
Where are you going to make the scenery?
Have you considered a backcloth?
Could you use slides as scenery?

Props

Who is going to oversee this aspect?
Make a list of all props required.
How will they be acquired?
Where will they be stored?
Check props supplied by children.
Have you the materials to make props?
Who is going to make them?
Do you need to make duplicates?
Can you replace disposable props?
Who is going to oversee props during the
    performance?
Are the props arranged near the set?
Have you got a props table or box?
Is there a list of props movements, scene by
    scene?
After the performance, check that all the
    props have been returned.

Costume

Who is going to oversee this aspect?
Make a list of characters and their costumes.
How much costume can be acquired?
How much will need to be made?
Can you resource it?
Storing finished costumes.
Is it period costume?
Is there a basic design?
What material will be appropriate?
Have you considered colour schemes?
Give children time to practise with
    'unusual' costumes.
Is the headgear secure?
What about feet?
Try to avoid hiring.

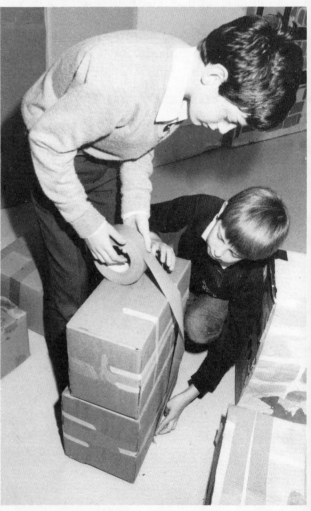

How will you construct your scenery?

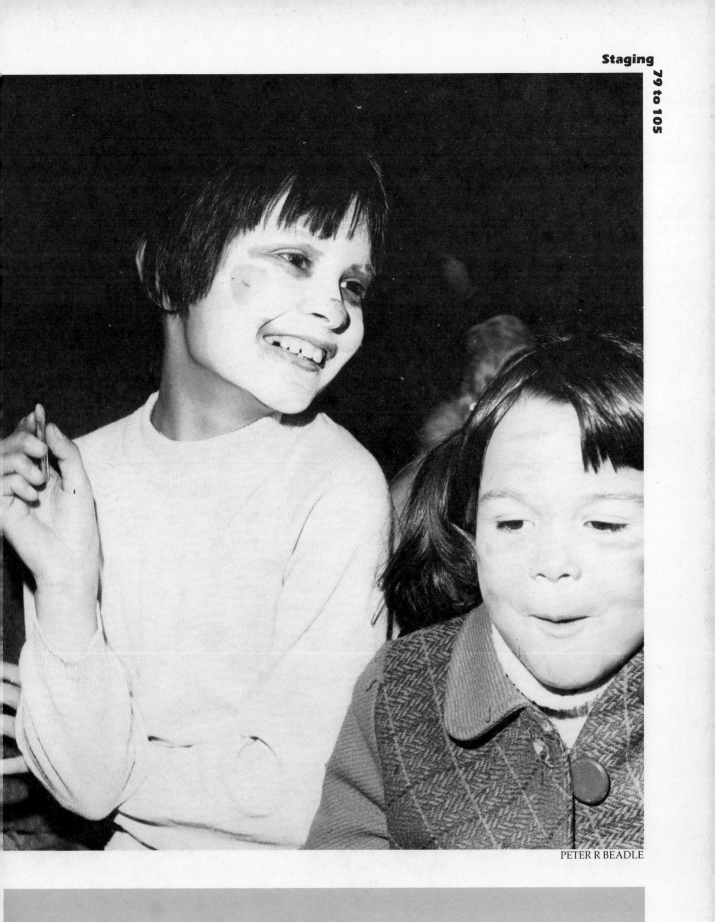

PETER R BEADLE

Staging

Staging

INTRODUCTION

RAYMOND IRONS

Now that the type of performance has been chosen, rehearsals are under-way, and scenery, costume and props are being made, your next major consideration will be staging. Now is the time to make final decisions concerning:

- performance venue and stage design,
- type of staging,
- entrances, exits, and movements,
- make-up,
- sound effects,
- lighting.

Stage design and siting

Where will it be held?

You are fortunate (and possibly unique) if your choice of venue is wide, for in many schools the hall, a classroom or simply a large, open space is your only option.

If you have a choice, you need to assess the different areas with regard to your script.

Points to consider

Where will your performance be staged most effectively? Are you anticipating a large or small audience?

Consider the acoustics (inside and out, since there may be more traffic noise near one area than another). How will the performers get to the performing area? Are there adequate entrances and exits? Is there sufficient performing space?

Wander round the area. If it is indoors look at the sides of the room from different angles, and try to judge where to situate your stage or performing area.

Some schools have permanent

staging, and so there is less flexibility in arranging the room. You could choose to ignore the built-in stage, of course, and use it for seating instead. The position of doors, windows, PE equipment, service hatches, linked classrooms, sinks, roof beams for lighting, electric points, and so on, will affect the positioning of the performing area.

Remember that, whichever room you choose, it is used five days a week or more, for regular aspects of school life. Your performance will only happen once a term (perhaps once a year) and the venue needs to reflect the excitement and help create the feeling of 'theatre'.

So try to create a different atmosphere by, for example, a change of backwall or the erection of rostra into a stage.

Stage design

In considering the stage design, you have a number of options.

End stage

This is probably the type of staging that parents envisage when invited to a

81

performance at school.

The stage is at one end of the room with the audience seated in straight rows directly facing the stage.

Unless the stage or the audience is elevated or raked, it becomes difficult to see from beyond the second row.

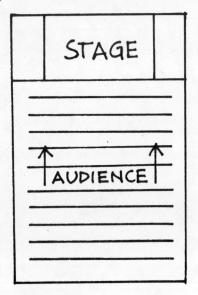

Open-end stage

This is a variation on the end stage where the stage area goes across the whole width of the room.

Another variation has curved seating. It is more suitable for the end stage arrangement as you may seat some of the front row with their backs to an open-end stage presentation. And your performance isn't that bad – is it?

Peninsular or thrust stage

This arrangement has the stage jutting out into the audience, which is seated on three sides. This may well increase the seating capacity and visibility.

Shakespeare's plays were first performed on a peninsular stage at the Globe Theatre which, it is said, held 3,000 people!

To provide a variation on the peninsular theme, place the jutting-out stage across a corner. A square-shaped room would lend itself more to this arrangement than a rectangular room.

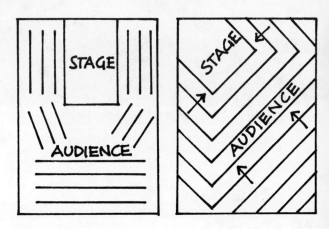

Transverse stage

With the transverse stage, the audience sit along two sides of the performing area. If children form the audience, watch out for face pulling and unwanted gestures across the divide!

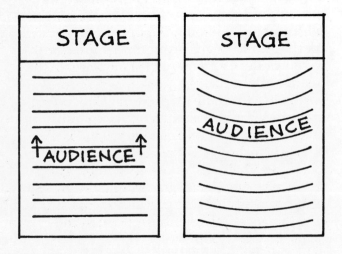

Theatre in the round or arena stage

This type of stage design has become popular for many types of performance. The stage area, which can be virtually any shape, is surrounded by the audience, and performers enter and exit through the audience, giving a feeling of nearness to and involvement with the performance.

Depending upon the nature of your performance, this type of staging could provide difficulties, and unless the stage is elevated or the audience raked, visibility can be a problem.

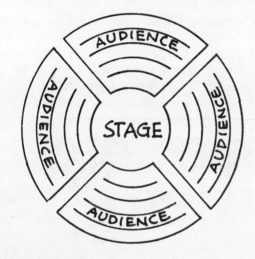

Multi-area stage

This can be a most effective way of staging your performance, especially if you are not anticipating a large audience. With lights to highlight each area as it is being used, you can set up, say, three different scenes.

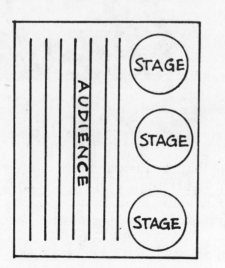

Points to consider

Whilst deciding on the design of staging there are a number of points to take into account:

● The audience needs to be able to see and hear clearly, otherwise the performance loses a great deal of purpose.

● The performers need to be able to enter and leave the stage area safely and properly. Access to the stage area is therefore a vital aspect of staging, and you need to consider the assembly area prior to coming into the audience's view. Some types of staging lend themselves more to this than others.

● Unless your audience comprises children who can sit on mats at the front, with benches and chairs towards the back, thereby creating a raked effect, then either the stage area or some of the audience will need to be raised. Some schools manage to create an amphitheatre effect by using rostra blocks to raise the audience who then look down on the stage area. This is more natural than raising your head up to an elevated stage.

You might be able to manage without either the stage area or the audience being raised if you are catering for a small audience and only require four or five rows of chairs. Beyond that, visibility does become a problem.

● The positioning of aisles is important. A central aisle can take out a considerable number of seats with good visibility, especially if you decide upon the end stage arrangement.

● Few primary schools have stage curtains and the traditional proscenium arch type of staging, so you need not consider this aspect unless, of course, your production would benefit from a form of curtaining.

A curtain proved most effective for the production of an old-time music hall. We constructed it between two PE apparatus support beams with brackets for the pulley system attached to the ceiling, and curtains which were already in use in school. The two Masters of Ceremony were positioned on the audience's side of the curtains and kept the whole show moving whilst the curtains were closed.

Curtains can have the advantage of

scenes and sets being prepared out of sight but can also have the disadvantage of fragmenting the performance and slowing it down.

● If you are using scenery, be it flats, boxes or backcloths, some stage arrangements lend themselves to it more than others. Scenery for a production in the round can be tricky!

● How will props arrive on stage? How will they depart? If the production is in the round, props will need backs and sides as well as fronts!

● How much performing area can be created? With your cast of thousands all crowding on stage for the finale, you need enough room to cater for all those bodies.

● If yours is a built-in stage, consider using a few rostra blocks to create an apron which will take the performance that bit closer to the audience.

● Avoid, at all costs, siting the stage area in front of windows, especially a large expanse of window. This is particularly off-putting in the daytime, when the audience is distracted by what is going on outside and by the light streaming through the window, which can be quite blinding on a bright day. You may also find that on a sunny day, having closed the curtains to keep out the sunlight, the temperature soars and you need to open the windows. This instantly creates a draught which in turn blows the curtains all over the performers. Keep away from windows!

● Staging a performance out of doors will create its own special problems. However, if you can locate a natural stage or a raised audience area then a major problem is solved. Depending upon the type of performance chosen, be prepared to move some equipment to the outdoor site. A parent may have a van or lorry which could be made available for this free of charge, but it would be as well to include hiring charges for transport in your budget.

Creating your stage

Whilst considering the different staging possibilities, you will also be thinking about what to use to create that staging.

Rostra blocks

Rostra blocks provide considerable flexibility in creating your stage. If your school doesn't possess any, it is well worth acquiring some. Try the local authority first – perhaps the drama or English adviser. Failing that, try the parents/parent-teacher/school association. There may even be a parent who can get the timber cheap and a group of parents who would construct the blocks. There are also a number of suppliers which provide rostra blocks.

You may be able to acquire them from your local secondary school or a neighbouring primary school but give them good warning, for often they are in use regularly.

Use a variety of blocks

A variety of blocks will again add to the flexibility, so go for different sizes and heights. You can then create different levels of staging which will add a further dimension to the audience's perspective and help to break up the flatness of a single level performance.

Steps are relatively straightforward to create with a variety of blocks, and if you can build a simple bannister, you can create the effect of a staircase leading off the stage.

We have the following selection which caters for up to 150 children in our productions: ten 120cm by 90cm by 45cm blocks; six 90cm by 60cm by 60cm blocks; and four 90cm by 30cm by 30cm blocks.

They are of permanent construction and stack away easily when not in use. Blocks could also be made to fold away. Remember that they will at times be supporting a considerable weight and must therefore be adequately reinforced.

Use rostra blocks to get just the right height.

The pieces of wood that form the surface need to fit snugly so that there is no movement, and you may wish to add temporary stiffeners to the corners.

Cuboid-shaped blocks will form the basis of your staging. Circular and semi-circular blocks will give much flexibility whilst ramps will solve the problem of small children getting on to a high stage area.

When you have decided upon the design of your stage area and have positioned the blocks, make a sketch of the arrangement, and include on each block shape the dimensions, or 'large', 'medium', 'small' etc.

This, together with pieces of coloured sticky tape on the floor to give you a guide, will save time in resiting your stage.

Getting used to the stage

As with costume and props, the earlier that children can use the stage the better, for movements, entrances and exits need practising until they become natural.

If your performance includes dance routines try to stage rehearsals right from the outset, or at least know the stage area and shape and mark it out on the floor. Otherwise the entire choreography will be affected and the routine may well have to be totally rethought when the stage is used.

Moving the staging

If you are using rostra blocks and creating your own stage design, decide upon the basic stage arrangement very early on in the project and rehearse on it from the beginning if possible, even if this means 'striking' (dismantling) the stage after each rehearsal and stacking it away. It will be a good activity for the stage-hands, as it will build up their muscles and get them in trim!

Remember to either supervise this yourself or ask a colleague to do so. There are safe and unsafe ways of moving this type of equipment and children need to be taught how to do it properly. Show them the safe way to bend and lift bulky, heavy equipment.

If you feel at all dubious about giving this task to the children, or if they are

Make sure children get used to the stage early on, especially if dancing is involved.

obviously too young, ask the caretaker or colleagues to do the job with you. Most children will be keen to do the job without fully realising the possible dangers and hazards.

Once the staging can be left permanently in position, there are two jobs to be done:
● secure the whole stage area so that it doesn't move when in use,
● 'Dolbyfy' the stage, ie create a noise reduction system.

Securing the stage

With rostra blocks there will be unavoidable movement when the children are on stage. If any movement more energetic than a slow walk takes place, the blocks will start to move apart leaving gaps. This, of course, can be a considerable hazard and could even lead to injury which will certainly cause a major disruption if it happens during a performance.

Using a rope

There are a number of ways to secure the staging, one of the easiest and quickest being to tie them together with a rope. Tie the rope around the outside of the blocks as

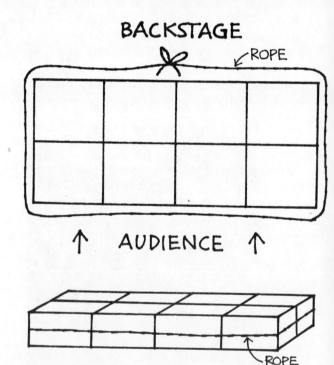

tight as possible with the knot at the back of the stage. Pieces of coloured paper stapled on to the blocks would hide the rope.

This works remarkably well and keeps the whole stage quite stable. You will need to check the tightness of the rope periodically in case it slackens.

86

Wood battens or wedges

A similar method is to secure battens of wood to the blocks – not necessarily all the way round, but just to secure one block to the next.

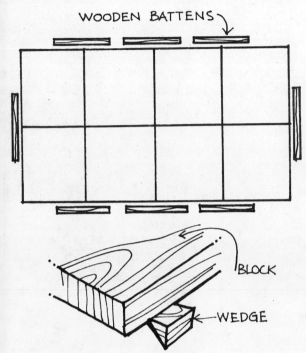

This is likely to take longer than the 'rope trick' but should not require checking, unless you attach balsa battens, in which case they will probably split when the stage is first used!

Wedges could do the job effectively, but again will need periodic checking. As they protrude out from the blocks, wedges could be a hazard, since children could trip over them and knock them out of position.

A floor guide

A floor guide might be a solution. This

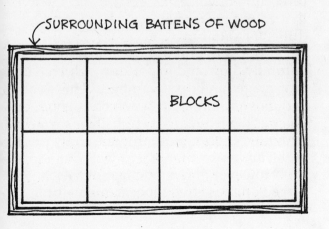

requires battens of wood around the perimeter of your stage area, secured to the floor.

However, this could result in double trouble:

● A floor may be a concrete base with thermoplastic tiles, in which case you will need masonry nails or a strong glue. This could create a further problem when you come to take up the guide after the final performance.

● The floor may be wooden and the 'powers that be' (ie caretaker and cleaners) may be extremely proud of its condition. Nailing or screwing or attacking it in any other way would be nothing short of treason, punishable by non co-operation from the entire caretaking and cleaning staff!

Noise reduction

As you can imagine, a number of children moving on rostra blocks will create a considerable noise level which can be quite distracting to the audience, so 'Dolbyfying' is a necessity.

Carpeting the rostra

It is usual to cover the rostra firstly with felt, and then a layer of canvas, which is stretched and nailed or tacked down.

Some commercially manufactured rostra have a carpet-type covering. If yours haven't, put out an appeal for carpet off-cuts. Always leave a border of carpet which can be turned over the edge of the block and tacked underneath or at the side. This prevents the edge becoming frayed or knocked up, both of which can become safety hazards.

Alternatively, carpet tiles are useful. When the block staging is in its final, permanent position, tack the tiles on to the surface. Tacking them across the blocks has the effect of joining blocks together, ensuring that there is no movement.

You may be fortunate enough to acquire a large piece of carpet that covers the whole stage area. This will also act as a stabiliser when tacked down.

The difference in noise level between carpeted and non-carpeted rostra is quite remarkable.

Entrances, exits and movements

A most important aspect of your stage design is how the children get on and off. If you have a raised stage, entrances and exits must look natural; steps should be incorporated so that they don't have to 'climb' on to the stage.

Where are the children coming from and how do they get to the stage area?

If children are arriving in pairs or small groups, is there sufficient room for them to get on stage?

Are the aisles wide enough or will the effect be spoiled by having to move singly or brushing into every member of the audience sitting next to the aisle?

Will you be creating wings at the side of the stage? If so, what purpose will they serve? For some types of staging design, wings are both inappropriate and impossible.

Looking 'natural'

Always bear in mind the relationship between performers and audience, since this is what the performance is all about. The nearer the performers are to the audience the less exaggerated the projection of voice and gesture – an aspect that young performers sometimes find difficult to attain.

The younger the child, the more naturally they tend to perform, which has its advantages and disadvantages. They look and move very naturally which is good, but voice and gesture projection are also natural and often cannot be heard or seen by most of the audience.

However, if too much emphasis is placed on these two aspects, the natural element begins to disappear as the children try to concentrate on saying their lines loudly. You must achieve a balance.

Backstage

In all backstage or off-stage areas, try to create as much space as possible and then define each area – for bulky props, scene change equipment, props table, sound effects, and so on. You need to create backstage a sense of calm and being in control of every situation, for this will be a great help to the children at performance time.

The type of room in which your performance is to take place may have little scope for a backstage area, and children will still be in view of the audience when they're not on the stage area. The audience will quickly accept this and may in their minds 'blank out' the sides of the stage.

However, the children need to be aware of how distracting it would be for the audience if there were any talking or fussing or unnecessary moving about.

Explain that when they are not on stage, they become part of the audience and should take a great interest in what's happening on stage, even though they

probably know the performance backwards!

The same applies to a chorus or crowd positioned at the side of the stage for part of the performance.

Once the children are on stage and the performance is under-way, there are many other aspects of stage craft to be considered.

Positions and moves

Position on the stage area can be helpful to the performer's projection. Once you know the area of stage the children will be using, plan out the positions and moves. Small or particularly large stage areas provide quite a challenge, so bear this in mind when designing the stage!

The movements and positioning are important because, just as a monotonous voice quickly loses the interest of the listener, so a static presentation will quickly lose your audience.

However, too much movement with little purpose is confusing. If it looks or feels awkward, change it.

All movements must come out of the script and move the performance forward. They can set a mood, develop an emotion, change a situation and create a different

Try to maintain a relaxed atmosphere backstage as this will help children who suffer from nerves.

focal point for the audience.

Try to use as much of the stage area as possible to keep the audience's eyes moving and to include the whole audience. When a critical or poignant moment arrives, stillness will accentuate the movement, especially if there has been a good use of movement previously.

You may need to group or regroup a number of characters and this needs to look natural. Get the children to 'talk' to each other (mime intelligently with no vocal sound) as they regroup, working them in pairs or small groups, so that the move is unobtrusive.

Children will tend to deliver their lines from the point where they enter the stage area, and to turn their backs as they speak to another character. Explain that the audience will not catch their lines and reposition the characters so that the one who is speaking can face the audience.

Stage areas

It might be helpful to divide your stage into areas; the children soon get the idea of stage right or left and upstage right or down-stage left. Remember that stage right is stage left to the audience and vice versa.

Include the whole audience and keep their attention

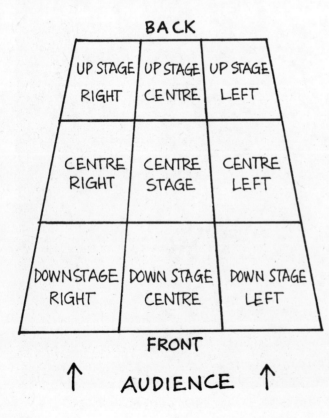

Points to remember

There are one or two points about stage position and movement which will help you and the children:

• Try to prevent a character from moving whilst speaking. Children's voices don't carry well (except on the playground of course), and the sound will dissipate quickly when they are moving. Also it helps the audience to understand what is being said if they can see the lip shape and facial expression of the speaker. So try to plan any movement between lines or during a natural pause.

• Move each character so that all sections of the audience see and hear as much of him or her as possible.

That is not to say that the characters should be facing the audience all the time, but there will be moments when a character needs to state an important line or to take the audience into his or her confidence and therefore needs to face the audience fully.

• If two characters are in conversation they don't need to face each other continuously or maintain constant eye contact. To do so would look awkward, so turn the characters slightly towards the audience.

● Positioning a character further down-stage makes them stronger and more dominant, but take care not to let them turn to speak to someone upstage, for then the roles are reversed and the upstage character who is facing the audience becomes dominant. This is known as 'upstaging'.

Also, the centre third of the stage tends to be stronger than the outer thirds, whilst stage right tends to be stronger than stage left. This will help you to plan moves more effectively.

● Consider the positioning of entrances, if you have a choice. Upstage entrances give a much stronger effect because the characters will be facing the audience fully on entry. This effect can be greatly lessened if a prop or character is positioned directly in front of the entrance and has to be negotiated by everyone who comes on. So for a really strong entrance have a clear access from an upstage position to a down-stage position.

Although down-stage is a strong area, a character entering down-stage will be in profile to the audience, which is not as strong as a full-face position.

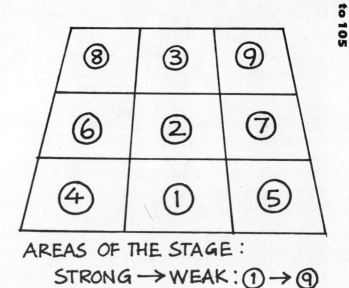

AREAS OF THE STAGE :
STRONG → WEAK : ① → ⑨

● By using the weaker areas of the stage it is possible to isolate characters whilst the main action continues. During *Jackie and the BEANSTALK Game*, the giant was 'sleeping' quite unobtrusively in area nine (upstage left) whilst all hell was let loose as Dracula, Frankenstein and skeletons danced and cavorted about in areas four, two, one

The actors needn't face the audience all the time, but they must do so for important movements or lines.

The giant sleeps upstage left while the audience's attention is on the characters in the stronger areas.

and five. It wasn't until the giant rose up and moved to area two that the audience realised he was there!

Rostra blocks which create different levels on the stage can also be strong areas. Even without blocks on a level stage, different heights can be created by the performers – some sitting, some kneeling and others standing. This is especially useful in a crowd scene, which can become overwhelming and confusing for the audience if everyone is standing all the time.

When you go through the script to plan movements and positions, mark key lines. Then, during rehearsal, check that the characters take up strong positions for their key lines.
● Try to avoid the characters standing in straight lines – unless you are presenting something with a military flavour. A straight line of actors can look quite odd to the audience.
● Diagonal moves tend to be stronger than

across the stage, with possibly the strongest being from upstage left to down-stage right.

When a group of characters move, the dominant one should move in front of the others to reach their destination first. Where the destination is another character, the dominant one may move behind or weave in and out of other characters before reaching the right place. In this case, they should complete their move before delivering their line so that the line gathers in importance; if the line comes before the move, it is the move which becomes more important.

If more than one character moves at the same time, and the moves cross over each other, it can become confusing to the audience.
● Don't feel that you have to stick too closely to published moves that accompany a printed script. Very often they are only brief suggestions, reflecting one person's interpretation, and no two productions of the same script will be the same.

Prepare the movements

You may wish to sketch the moves of each character. If this is too time-consuming, jot one or two notes down rather than plotting major moves, entrances and exits at rehearsal while the children are left twiddling their thumbs awaiting the decisions. In other words, prepare each rehearsal and have in your mind at least the general pattern of movements for that rehearsal. If the children sense that you are badly prepared, their approach and attitude may well begin to change and sloppiness will start to creep in. Also you will be wasting their valuable playground time which they have kindly given up in the interests of putting on a performance!

Prepare the basic moves before the rehearsals.

Make-up

Is make-up really necessary? What effect will it have on the performance for audience and performers? If we decide to use make-up, who can I ask to deal with it? Is there anyone with prior knowledge of make-up? Why is make-up used?

Answering this final question may help you to answer the rest.

Make-up is used to make the faces of the performers look right for the production. This can mean a host of different guises or just a very simple minimum covering.

Stage lights tend to make a performer's face look pale and flatten the features. With

93

properly applied make-up, both of these problems can be put right.

Where the performers are taking on a very different type of character (such as an old person, a person of different nationality, a villain or a clown), make-up will add realism.

Make-up can also evoke reactions and emotions. If applied well, it will add considerably to the audience's appreciation, but poorly applied make-up will detract from the performance, in which case it is far better to avoid make-up at all.

Most children enjoy painting their faces and some are quite expert at it. You may well find that a number of children have their own make-up equipment and are more than willing to bring it into school and use it. (A publication worth investing in is *Make Up for Fun* by Patric Parmentier. It develops in themes, giving make-up plans for animals, clowns, landscapes and old age, as well as hints about what to use, how to apply it and how to remove it.)

PETER R BEADLE

Most children love painting their faces.

94

Who can help?

If you decide to use make-up, find out whether any parents or friends have some expertise in stage make-up. Have you any contacts in local theatre groups who would come along to school and explain a little about stage make-up to you, your colleagues and the children? Even your local television station may provide information, advice and maybe even a visiting expert.

The amount of make-up used by the vast majority of your cast will probably be minimal, so you could teach the chorus or crowd to apply their own make-up, freeing you, colleagues or parents to concentrate on the more demanding faces.

If there are parents willing to assist with make-up, it will be a great help if they come into school before performance day to practise. This is essential for character or fantasy make-up, for you will be lucky to arrive at the right effect ten minutes before the character appears on the stage.

Organise a make-up afternoon when children, teachers and parents can experiment and practise until a satisfactory result appears. Try to arrange this quite well into the project, so that costumes can be tried on and make-up matched.

What is available?

Your choices of make-up are seemingly endless, as any venture into the realms of a department store would confirm.

However, you will probably turn to either Max Factor or Leichner, a combination of both, or face paints.

Start with creams of foundation make-up or the traditional Leichner grease-paint sticks. Different make-up artists have developed their own preferences for which type to use, and will often choose a mixture of both.

A basic foundation make-up comprises a Max Factor Satin Smooth basic colour tube (say 25 or 26) and powder. For a grease-paint foundation, mix Leichner No 5 (a deep, creamy colour) and No 9 or No 8 (reddish-brown) and add powder.

With these foundations, the natural skin colouring will be hidden, and under lights this gives a flattening effect.

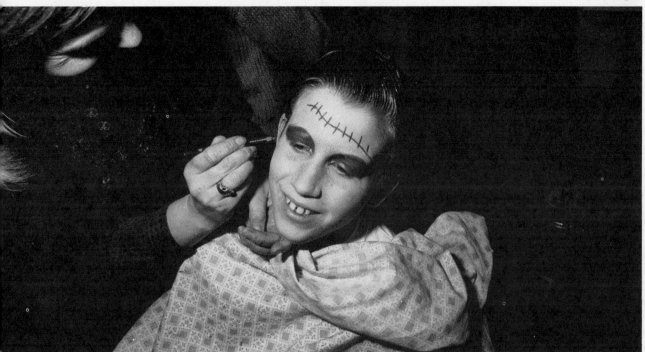

Practise applying make-up, especially if it is to look striking, and remember to protect clothing.

Highlights and shadows are therefore needed in order to recreate the shape and structure of the face. For highlighting, the Leichner No 5 stick is useful, whilst a Leichner No 25 (cake liner) is suitable for shadow effects as well as for character make-up. These can be used with or without foundation.

For eyes and mouth any black or brown eye-liner and suitable lipstick will be quite adequate.

Creating different effects

In school productions, the audience is often very close to the performers, so make-up needs to be extremely well applied and subtle.

However, with character or fantasy make-up, the rules of subtlety do not apply; accentuated features and exaggerated make-up can give a tremendous boost to the overall effect. Eye shape in particular can give a most striking effect.

Wherever make-up is applied, add a light dabbing of powder to set the make-up, brushing off any surplus.

Greying the hair can be achieved by adding streaks of white grease-paint or shaking on talc. (Don't sprinkle the talc too

liberally or there will be white clouds every time the head is moved sharply!)

With a modern production you may include striped, tartan, Union Jack or chessboard hair! In our production of *Hardy Annuals* and *Jackie and the BEANSTALK Game*, certain characters had punk hair styles. The children chose the style and colouring themselves and, with our approval, applied their own hair make-up. This type of make-up helped the performers to 'get into' their characters in a most convincing way.

Remember that the performers need to be in their costumes *before* any make-up is applied, otherwise taking off or putting on vests, T-shirts and jumpers will ruin the make-up. The performers will also need protective clothing so that their costumes are not made up as well as their faces.

Removing make-up

For taking off make-up, both Max Factor and Leichner produce removal creams, but any commercially produced cleansing cream or face cream will do.

First remove the heavier make-up with tissue. Then rub in some removal cream until a rather unpleasant 'mush' develops. Remove this with tissues, then use a good soap and hot water wash to see off any remaining make-up. Ensure that the children do not rub any cream into their eyes.

Check beforehand whether any of the performers are unable to use make-up because of a skin condition, or because it creates an unpleasant reaction. Water-based make-up or children's face paints may be more acceptable, but if there is any doubt, don't use any.

Think before you buy

If you need to buy make-up, don't forget to budget for it and include it in the initial financial discussions.

Like costume and scenery, make-up will add a further dimension to the production, but it will not hide basic flaws in the direction or acting ability of the performers.

Finally, with many children, especially younger ones, make-up may not be necessary at all, particularly when there are no stage lights and where no distinctive characters are involved. So don't feel pressurised into using make-up, for as Philippe Perrottet says in his book *Practical Stage Make Up*, 'the less that is done to a child's face on the stage, the better'.

PETER R BEADLE

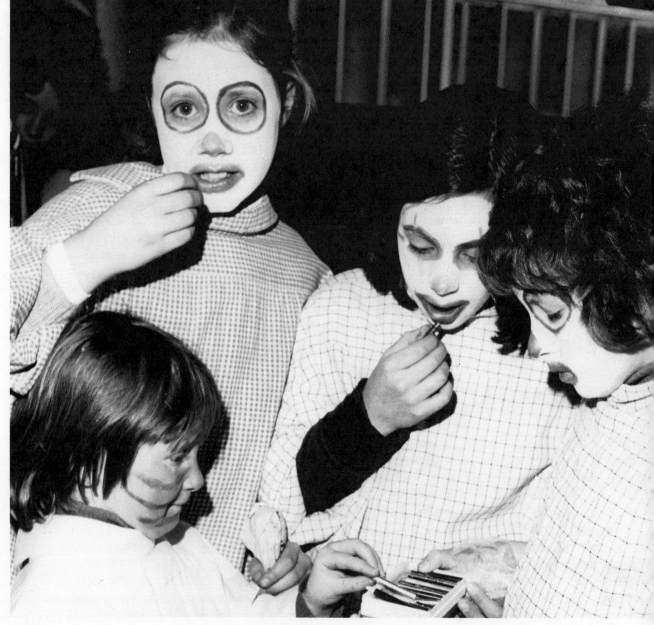

Children's face paints are just as effective as make-up and may be gentler on young sensitive skin.

Sound and sound effects

What sounds are needed?

Sound and other effects may not be essential for a successful performance, but assuming that through your now well practised powers of flattery, persuasion or blatant bribery, you have found a 'volunteer' to take charge of effects, go through the script together, marking where sound and sound effects are required.

Discuss the type of sound:
- How appropriate is it to the action?
- Is it absolutely necessary?
- Will the audience appreciate it?
- Will it be live or recorded?
- Could you use a microphone?
- What amplification and speaker capacity is available?

For recorded sounds, cassette players are easy to operate – use a separate cassette for each sound.

How can they be achieved?

Having decided what effects are needed, discuss with a small group of sound engineers (children) how these sounds can be made. With short sound effects, such as a door knocker or bell, thunder or a telephone, always try to create them live every time. The timing problems that can occur with recorded short sound effects can often ruin a scene.

Also try to situate the sound close to the source on stage, and direct the performers to turn or look towards the sound. This helps the audience to focus on the sound quickly.

Recording the sounds

Where it is necessary to record the sounds or use a recorded source, consider the following points:
● Always check the copyright and performing rights.
● Try to avoid a record-player; a cassette-player is much easier to operate.
● A reel-to-reel tape-recorder would be even better, since it is easier to edit and splice a tape than a cassette, and you have more control.
● Make sure you have a back-up machine in case of breakdowns.
● Check the counter (not all machines count at the same speed) and note down the counter number for the start of each effect.
● Try to record on the play-back machine.
● You could use a separate cassette for each sound so that they can be set accurately, depending on the number of cassettes you can find.
● Label each side of the tape or cassette, even if only one side is used.
● Use the pause button and volume control to fade a sound, otherwise you will hear machine clicks.
● If you need recorded music before the performance and between scenes, always record considerably more than you need – just in case!
Record sound effects in a quiet room so that unwanted sounds do not creep on to the recording.

By subtle use of the volume control, you can make planes, cars or trains pass by. Simply increase and decrease either the volume output, or the volume input if you are recording these sounds live.

There are plenty of commercially produced sound effects records and cassettes which you may find in your local public library, in case there is not enough time to devise your own.

Practical considerations

Check the balance and level of sound from different positions in the audience area. Is the background music too loud or soft? Do short sound effects create the right effect? Remember that sound will be absorbed more quickly and effectively when the audience is present.

Check all the following points:
● How near to an electric point is the sound equipment situated?
● Have you sufficient extension cables, both in quantity and length?
● Have you an adequate stock of adaptors?
● Have you labelled the plugs and corresponding adaptor sockets?
● Have you spare fuses of the correct ampage?
● Who can change a plug – correctly!
● Have you allocated specific areas backstage for your sound engineers, and have they an adequate view of the performing area – this is critical for live sound effects.
● Has the chief sound engineer got a set of sound cues marked on his or her script?
● If you are going to use microphones, are they meant to amplify the general noise level or to be used by specific performers?
● Will the microphones be on a stand, plus boom, or hand-held? If they are hand-held, what happens to them when they are finished with?

Sound and sound effects probably have the greatest potential for going wrong, so don't be tempted to complicate your ever-growing problems with too much sophistication. Keep it simple!

For sound and lighting equipment, set aside specific areas backstage and take care with trailing leads.

Lighting

Many of the points relating to sound and sound effects could also be asked of lighting.

Why do you need lighting? The obvious reason is that it enables the audience to see the performers and the action more clearly, but it can also create different moods, atmospheres and effects.

Can you manage without lighting? This will depend to some extent upon when your performance is to take place. Daytime will produce its own natural light which can

range from brilliant sunlight to a rather dull murky twilight. Unfortunately this is one aspect of the project that cannot be planned.

However, even with the state of education today, the vast majority of schools will have electricity and therefore some in-built form of lighting.

In many halls and classrooms, it is possible to light just the performing area with the ceiling lights and, for an evening performance with curtains closed, this form of lighting will be quite adequate.

Additional lighting

If you choose to bring in additional lighting, consider whether the venue for your performance is suitable to house lights safely. Is there sufficient hanging space near the performing area for lights?

There may be beams which form part of the structure of the room or PE support beams to which lights could be attached safely. This is preferable to floor standing lights which, in order to be effective, need to be mounted on a fairly tall stand.

It is essential that you find the school fuse box and check the maximum load that can be used, since this will dictate just how many lights (and appliances) you can safely use.

What is available?

Check what resources you have or can acquire, always assuming that the school's electrical capacity can cope with this extra load.

Lights (or luminaires, as they are sometimes referred to) are generally available in four wattages – 500, 750, 1000 and 2000. You will probably find that 500W bulbs are quite adequate for your purposes, and you can use twice as many 500W as 1000W bulbs.

There are many kinds of lighting available but, for school purposes, these divide into two basic sections – spotlights and floodlights.

Spotlights

Spotlights are used primarily to light the performers. There are two types:
● Spots or profile spots produce a very intense, hard-edged beam of light of a fixed size. These are the ones that you try not to look at directly and which produce 'oohs' and 'aahs' from the children when lights are used for the first time.
● Fresnel spots produce a soft-edged beam of light which is directional; they are excellent for lighting certain areas of the stage as well as performers.

Floodlights

Floodlights are used to 'flood' the performing area with light and are also divided into two types:
● Floods are of low intensity, producing a wide-angled beam of light. They can be single lights or a number joined together to form a batten.
● Footlights are used to throw light up at the performers from floor level but are used less often today.

Special effects

Your lighting will probably fall into one or all of the first three of the four categories above.

A profile spotlight produces a hard-edged light to focus attention on a small area of the stage.

Beyond these, you may feel that special effects would add greatly to a scene or part of a scene.

Strobes

Strobes (stroboscopic lights) will give a flashing light effect and can be most effective. However, they should only be used for short periods because they can induce an unbalancing experience, hurt the eyes and, in extreme cases, cause an epileptic fit. In some areas there are legal requirements regarding strobes, so if you are thinking of using one it would be wise to check.

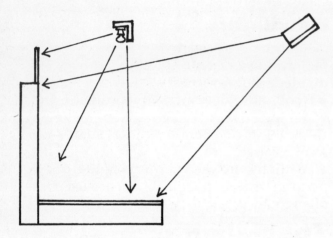

Lighting plan seen from the side.

Ultraviolet

Ultraviolet light can also be very effective, picking out in a darkened area those items which are specially treated or painted. It needs to be timed and switched on a little before it is needed as it becomes effective only gradually.

Wheels

Wheels attached to spots can have a dual function. With coloured gels over the holes you can save on the number of lights you need. They can also double as a strobe by leaving the holes uncovered and rotating the wheel, creating a strobe-type effect. If you use the wheel for this, do make sure that it is fixed securely to the light.

Colour filters

Jellies or gels are colour filters made of gelatine slides, usually mounted in a frame, which are slipped over the lenses of the lights. They are available commercially in a wide range of colours, and are likely to be made of a thin plastic or Cellophane nowadays.

If you decide to make your own lights out of tins or cans, a piece of coloured Cellophane can be taped across the end of the tin. Remember to drill sufficient holes in the base of the tin to provide ventilation and so avoid the casing becoming too hot.

Gels are used to give tone or atmosphere to the set, overcoming the clinical effect of 'white' light. However, if you have a very limited number of lights (say one or two), it would be better not to use gels for they can cut down the amount of light considerably. The more lights you have, the more you can experiment with the effects of different-coloured gels.

Controlling brightness

A light-coloured or white background set will become extremely bright under lights and could take the audience's eye away from the performers and the action. A dark background will not look bright under lights, but will highlight the performers.

A dimmer board can be most useful and can save a great deal of wear and tear on bulbs. It is simply a piece of equipment designed to dim or fade (or brighten) the lights. This saves the bulbs from a sudden

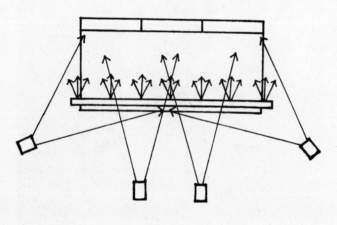

Lighting plan seen from above.

surge of current each time they are switched on. Remember to fade the lights to 'off' before switching the board on or off.

What is needed?

Early on in the project, whoever is taking on the lighting responsibility will need to go through the script with you and discuss the lighting needs. Even the obvious lighting points need to be jotted down scene by scene – time of day, mood of scene, when the lights go on and off, weather conditions, and so on.

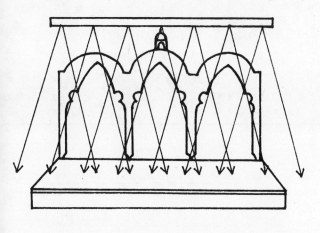

Lighting from an overhead baton.

The lighting person will also need to find out the general colours of the costumes and make-up as well as the scenery design and colour, and experiment (colours can look quite different once the lights are on).

Finding equipment

If you do not possess your own lighting equipment at school, there are many ways to get hold of some. But seek advice first. Your English or drama adviser may be able to help with advice on purchasing, or where lights can be borrowed from within the authority.

Neighbouring schools, primary and secondary, may be willing to loan equipment but book up in good time. Secondary schools, especially, may also have someone willing to help out with lighting on performance day. Always check with the heads of both your school and the

secondary school to make sure that this liaison is desirable.

You may have in your area a thriving amateur theatrical group, or even a theatre, which would be willing to loan out lighting equipment.

There are, of course, firms which hire out such equipment, too.

Checking equipment

The lighting person should make the following checks:
● Are the lights still in one piece? This check is especially necessary if you have borrowed or hired equipment. Make a list of the equipment and note any problems as soon as it arrives in school.
● Are the lenses clean?
● Is the cable in good condition?
● Are the plugs correctly fused and wired?
● Are there sufficient gels in a usable condition?
● Is there an adequate supply of spare fuses and bulbs?
● Are there enough adaptors to take all the plugs?
● Are the plugs and their respective sockets or points labelled?
● What is the state of the G/C clamps and safety chains?

Lights must be securely fixed to a support beam.

A fresnel spotlight gives a soft-edged beam of light for highlighting certain areas or characters.

- Does the dimmer board operate successfully?
- Are extension leads available?
- Is there adequate covering for cables eg small mats, or tape to secure cable to beams and floor?
- Are the stands for floor-mounted lights in sound condition? (Whilst on the subject of floor-mounted spots, avoid placing them too far back in the audience as their effect diminishes for the performers but could 'blind' the audience!)

Involving the children

If you intend to involve children in the lighting team, the potential dangers and safety hazards need to be explained carefully and seriously. If you have any misgivings about involving children in this aspect, don't! Lighting is potentially the most dangerous aspect of the project.

However, the children we have involved in our lighting team have taken their roles very seriously, and have carried them out in a most sensible way, showing a great capacity for safety awareness.

Lighting rehearsal

House lights may also be used during the performance.

If they are merely switched off at the beginning and on at the interval and end, then the cues are fairly straightforward. But if they are being used as a lighting effect during the performance, a cue sheet will be required.

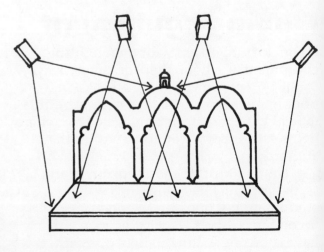

Floodlights either side with two central beams.

Do try to arrange a lighting rehearsal so that the lighting team can check cues etc, and the performers can start getting used to the lights.

As the first night is about to begin, there can be few moments more magical than when the house lights go down and the stage lights come up.

Checklist

Where will your performance be held?
Why has that venue been chosen?
Where will the performing area be?
What design will the performing area be?
Will all the audience be able to see?
What about aisles and curtains?
Will you be using rostra blocks?
Are the stage-hands organised?
Is the staging secure?
Is the stage 'Dolbyfied'? How?
Have you considered entrances and exits to and from the staging?
How much space can you create backstage?
Have you planned out the movements and positioning of large props?

Divide the stage into areas.
Are you conversant with the tricks of the trade – stagecraft?
Will make-up be used?
Is there sufficient in stock?
Who's taking responsibility for make-up?
How much sound and what sound effects will be used?
Check copyright conditions.
Who's taking responsibility for sound?
What resources are available?
Will lighting, apart from existing lights, be used?
Who's taking responsibility for lighting?
Have you adequate resources and equipment?
Is there sufficient capacity for your requirements?
Where will the lights be positioned?
Make stringent safety checks.
To what extent will children other than performers be involved in the aspects of staging?
To what extent will parents, friends of the school and the local community be involved in the aspects of staging?

Practical arrangements

Practical arrangements

INTRODUCTION

Any practical arrangements in preparation for the performance will probably fall into two areas:
● the ongoing planning that began the moment you had the crazy idea of putting on a performance,
● planning for the performance day itself, right up to the point when the 'curtain rises'.

There are some aspects that can be planned in advance, such as:
● advertising,
● tickets and programmes,
● invitations,
● recording the performance,
● catering,
● front-of-house arrangements,
● backstage arrangements.

Other aspects of the project which require planning will develop along the way. As producer and director you will be expected to have planned for everything, even to the extent of a contingency plan when two thirds of the chorus goes down with 'waffle over-indulgence' during lunch on dress rehearsal day.

Advertising

One aspect which needs thinking about early in the project is advertising.

An audience will take you straight into the realms of advertising, since they need to know certain basic facts, and your advertising needs to answer these questions clearly, briefly and attractively.

You will need to decide therefore who your advertising is aimed at:
- parents,
- ex-pupils,
- wider public and community.

You will also need to consider how much publicity is required, taking into account the seating capacity of the performance room.

Here are some ways you could publicise the performance:
- poster,
- handbills,
- newsletter,
- notice-board (in school, school gate),
- local shops,
- local paper,
- local radio and/or TV station,
- through the authority mailing to many schools.

And, of course, the children themselves are excellent publicity agents.

Having decided upon the type of advertising that best suits your project and resources, you will need to decide how the advertising material is to be produced. This will involve the methods of printing, the materials used, and the amount of time available.

If you decide to produce all the advertising material in school there are a number of methods you could use.

Making posters

The children could produce a poster, providing an opportunity for considerable discussion and research about the power of the advertisement.

Bring into the classroom posters and advertisements. Better still, ask the children to find an advertisement or poster that has caught their eye.

Discuss lettering, colour, shape and why certain advertisements are more eye-catching than others. Talk about the information that needs to go on your poster. Let the children experiment with different styles and shapes of lettering and different colour combinations.

Simply handing out a piece of plain paper, felts and crayons, with the relevant information displayed on the board or overhead projector, can often produce quite unrewarding results.

A poster competition

You may decide to hold a poster competition throughout the school, the winning entry being used on the advertising material.

Display the other entries all around school, or make a feature of them in the hall and entrance hall. This helps to focus the children's minds on the performance day.

Reproducing the posters

Photocopying a child's original poster can be relatively cheap (include their permissions and a credit, of course). Most school photocopying machines will make a good reproduction of a bold black and white original.

Drawing the original on to a duplicating skin or Banda skin is an alternative if a photocopier is not available. Generally speaking, however, the result will not be as good.

Some computer programs allow you to print out a poster, a programme and even your own newspaper article about the forthcoming production. This could be a way of interesting the local press by sending them a computer-produced press release and inviting them to send a cameraman to the dress rehearsal.

Protecting posters

Original posters will need a waterproof cover if they are to be displayed outside. A 'runny' poster is not the best advertisement

Designing a poster will encourage discussion of advertising techniques and eye-catching designs.

for your production! Use a layer of transparent contact, having mounted the poster on stiff card first, or laminate it, or simply put it inside a clear, plastic envelope to protect it from the elements – and large dogs.

Large, bold lettering using brightly-coloured felt-tip pens make eye-catching posters.

Printing handbills

Has your school got its own printing press? Some schools have invested in a press and produce fancy tickets and handbills for every imaginable function. It can be quite a source of revenue – but beware, it can also be extremely time-consuming and needs parental input on the labour side.

Perhaps a group of children could set a plate for a handbill and print it out themselves. Check the lettering, for it is very easy to mix up the characters and styles. Also demonstrate the inking process to the children, before they have a go!

Small handbills can be delivered to the local shops for display, and are cheap enough for every child to take home and display, too.

T-shirts and badges

As mentioned earlier in the costume section, you may decide to print a T-shirt as part of the costume, and this will be a form of advertising. If you can persuade a national high street store to purchase, for a phenomenal sum, a small area on the back of each T-shirt, then your financial

problems are solved!

What about producing your own badges, displaying some aspect of your project?

Badge-making machines are available to hire, but check on how many badges need to be sold and at what price in order to make a profit. This is a good mathematical problem for your class on Monday morning. You may, of course, know someone who owns such a machine or can obtain one cheaply. Some firms will produce badges for you, but again check the costs.

We hired a machine very cheaply from a friend of the school, and the children produced six designs which were then drawn in black and white to the correct size. The master copy was whisked along to the local teachers' centre and printed on different coloured paper.

The children simply cut out the individual circles and placed them, with the badge base and Cellophane, into the machine – and the badges were completed. (Remember to draw an outer circle on the master copy, otherwise the cutters will cut too close to the design, and there won't be sufficient paper to hold the badge together!)

The children will love to design their own badges.

111

Design a logo

Have you thought of designing a logo especially for the production? This could be incorporated in all your advertising material, as well as your invitations, and newsletters. It might be simply the school's initials, or perhaps a character or aspect from the production. Again, it will focus children's attention and add extra interest.

Printing out of school

Unless you have a contact in the printing business who will not charge you, then as soon as you take the production of advertising material out of school you will begin to incur costs.

Shop around your local printers, specify clearly your requirements, and ask for quotations for both the cost and the time taken to do the job. When accepting a quotation, do so in writing, itemising exactly what you understand the quotation to include, and keep a copy! Also check whether the school can reclaim the VAT charges through your local education authority.

Before going to the expense of a printing contract, however, check whether the local authority, resources centre, or teachers' centre have printing facilities.

These facilities provide excellent results, usually at cost, and you may even be able to charge the bill to capitation, thus relieving your very tight budget a little. Check this with the head, of course, so that the debit item 'Printing' in the next capitation print-out doesn't come as a complete surprise!

When do you start advertising?

This will depend to a large extent upon the scale of the project and who will form the audience.

Send a newsletter

As soon as the performance date is known, make a general announcement in a newsletter so that parents can book the date in their diaries. An early announcement is especially helpful if it is a Christmas production, for diaries become booked up quite early for the last week of the autumn term. This is particularly important if the audience is spread wider than children and parents of the school.

The main thrust of the advertising will probably begin two to three weeks before performance day. By this time you will have more details about the project and some little snippets of information about its progress to keep parents in touch.

Enlist the help of your school secretary or any other competent typist for schedules and newsletters.

Large events

For a larger event, perhaps a local schools' festival, begin the main thrust earlier – say a month before – and try to update the information in the local press each week. (Suggest articles about co-operation between a number of schools, links with the community, and perhaps the composer of the work being performed, or a photograph of rehearsals, highlighting a certain aspect of the festival.) You will need to advertise on a large scale for a schools' festival, since your overheads will be so much higher and you are aiming to attract the general public as well as parents.

You need to sell sufficient tickets to at least cover your costs, and involve the public in order to further develop school and community links.

Tickets and programmes

Tickets

Tickets are a receipt for money handed over, and can be seen as a commitment that the buyer will attend the function and that the seller will provide a seat in the case of a performance. Whether that seat is reserved is another matter.

You will need to keep a running total of the number of people planning to attend, so that you can put out the correct number of chairs and make sure you don't go beyond your maximum capacity. The maximum capacity will depend not only on how many chairs will fit into the hall, but also on fire regulations.

Information to include on the tickets

- name and address of school,
- title of the production,
- author and composer credits,
- dates,
- times,
- price (if applicable),
- refreshments (if applicable).

Programmes

It is always a good idea to hand out programmes as the audience arrives, or even distribute them beforehand. Theatre-goers expect to have some information on the production and the people involved which they can read through before the curtain rises, even if it is a simple, one-sided sheet of duplicated paper.

Information to include on the programmes

- name and address of school,
- title of production,
- author and composer credits,
- dates,
- times,
- scene headings,
- 'Thanks to . . .'

Other aspects you may be able to include:
- brief synopsis of the plot (omitting the ending, of course),
- cast list: the length will depend upon space available. Our programmes are usually A4, folded to give four sides of A5, and we have managed a cast list of 150 names on one of these sides. Include all the non-actors as well – stage-hands, front-of-house, band etc.

Designing the programme

A programme cover design competition right across the school will create interest and give every child the opportunity to participate. As with the poster, entries can be displayed around the school during the last two or three weeks of the project, so that children, parents and visitors to the school will be aware that something is happening.

You may even put a lucky number in a corner of the programme with a prize for the number drawn at some point in the performance – preferably not during the action!

Combining the two

An alternative to producing both tickets and programmes is to combine them and produce one article – a 'tickamme' or a 'procket'. This will save considerable time and possible expense. Where you are presenting more than one performance, print all the performances on the programme and, as orders 'flood in', cross

Programmes are a good idea and could even be combined with the ticket to save time and expense.

The children could take a retiring collection.

out the performances not required. Remember to keep a note of how many programmes have been distributed for each performance.

Dealing with money

If you decide to charge by selling tickets you will have to discuss the price. You may charge different rates for adults, children and OAPs, so all of these will need to be included on advertising material and the tickets. You may also decide to offer a family ticket at a reduced rate.

Set up a system

Ask someone to take charge of the 'box office' and let parents know when it is open. Perhaps the school secretary will take on this role. Alternatively, you may feel this is a role that a parent can oversee, or even a rota of parents. Again this is a practical way of involving parents, resulting in some personal advertising.

Whoever takes on the role will need a system for issuing tickets and collecting and banking money. Clear records of money received and banked will need to be kept for future audit purposes. It is always helpful to issue an information sheet about the 'box office' system, especially if a rota of people is involved.

Taking a collection

Another way of charging is to organise a retiring collection or silver collection. This simply means that, at the end of the performance, the audience puts into strategically placed collection plates (or buckets) an amount of money, which may well reflect their enjoyment and appreciation of the performance! (89 pence, six foreign coins, three buttons and a milk token really speak for themselves!)

This method, although less predictable, is far easier to administer. The performers can hold the receptacles, and all the money comes in at once. It can be counted, sorted, bagged and banked the same day or the next. With evening performances, decide what is going to happen to the money overnight. Your school safe is probably not insured for such large sums.

Where is the money going?

Whichever method of charging you choose, someone will ask where the money is going. Expenses should be covered by the takings, but you will have to decide what to do with any profit.

If you choose a worthy cause, the audience may even dig a little deeper into their pockets. You may decide on a charity, a specific school project or simply a rainy day.

Do let parents, and your wider audience if possible, know how much was eventually raised and what the money was used for. This may be included in a post-performance article to the local paper, the school newsletter, or even on a small handbill.

Sponsorship

The idea of sponsorship may have already been dismissed as a way to off-set some of your costs. However it need not be merely a way of obtaining financial support, but a way of building bridges with the local community and industry.

Many firms, shops and businesses allocate a weekly, monthly, or yearly advertising sum, and you may well find that an amount of money could be directed to the school from this fund. Some firms may prefer to offer their services or a raffle prize instead of an actual amount of money.

You could sell advertising space in the programme, but any offer of money from firms should be mentioned in the credits.

If there is a particular theme or topic which forms a major aspect of the production you could contact firms or businesses who deal in that particular product. *Jackie and the BEANSTALK Game* is focused around a computer and we contacted a well known international computer firm with offices in Warwick.

You may find that firms are willing to come to school to talk to the children about the work of their firm and its produce. A visit may be arranged to the firm and so links are established with local industry.

MARIA BARTHA

Invitations

Who to invite

The big problem with invitations is that someone will be left out! There's only room

for a certain number of people and, once the limit has been reached, the line must be drawn.

This may mean compiling a priority list

and, surely, top of that list must come the parents. It would be unthinkable to have a packed hall with some parents unable to get in because the entire town council and local WI have taken up all the seats.

The parents will receive their invitations via the children and the newsletter, and you will need to seat all parents who wish to attend.

If there are still seats available, you could invite any of the following:
- governors of the school,
- LEA officers,
- advisory staff,
- neighbouring schools,
- people who have helped towards the production,
- ex-staff and pupils,
- teachers' centre warden,
- visiting peripatetic staff,
- ancillary staff, kitchen staff, dinner ladies, cleaner, caretaker, crossing warden, classroom helper, educational assistant, secretary – people who are in daily contact with the children but not often recognised for the important jobs they do.

Performing for old people

At one school, we would always put on a special performance during an afternoon for two local old people's homes. Transport was arranged by the school to collect the old people, who were entertained, served with refreshments and then transported home at the end of the afternoon. For some, it was the only outing of the year, and the children learned about respect for others and giving their talents to others. There was also a considerable amount of parental involvement and help.

Producing the invitations

Ask the children to write out the invitations, including an RSVP. Children are quite thrilled to receive replies.

The format of the invitations will be similar to the poster and perhaps the same design and lettering could be used. They could even be hand-tinted to look more attractive. When you are sending invitations remember to budget for postage.

Reserving seats

If you intend to reserve seats, try not to offend anyone! I have seen performances where the whole of the front two rows have had reserved tickets put on them, and the occupants have arrived just as the curtain rises only to block the hitherto unrestricted view of the next two rows, which are usually filled by the younger brothers and sisters of the performers. Such insensitive

You could arrange for old people to be collected from a local home for a special performance.

117

reservation of seats can create bad feelings amongst parents.

On the other hand, if guests have been invited, you do not wish to seem discourteous by having no seats left for them.

If you are going to reserve seats for the guests, space them out around the hall and not necessarily in what are regarded as the best seats. If there are no reserved seats, it might be as well to let guests know this in advance.

Always try to have a member of staff and some children to act as ushers, greeting people at the door as they arrive. By doing this, the audience will feel welcome in the school and specially invited guests can be escorted into the hall.

Recording the performance

You may feel that so much time, effort and hard work (as well as enjoyment) have gone into the project that you'd like to make a recording of the performance. This can be achieved basically in two ways – audio and visual, a tape/cassette-recording and a video-recording.

Sound-recording

Your choice between audio and visual will be governed by the resources you either possess or can acquire. Your school will probably possess a cassette-recorder and a blank cassette, and so a sound-recording is possible.

Check that you have sufficient play time on the cassette. If you can arrange the interval just before the first side of the cassette finishes, you can change sides without losing any of the performance!

If this can't be done, you will lose a little of the performance during change-over time, unless you have two machines, in which case you merely start recording on the second machine just before the first cassette comes to an end. You can then do a simple editing job and produce a complete performance on cassette.

Video-recording

Making a video-recording of the performance requires more consideration.

Your school may not possess a video camera or a video machine, in which case you may be able to acquire one from a member of staff, a parent, a friendly school or the local authority, or you could rent one (requiring a hefty deposit).

Blank video-cassettes are much more expensive than sound-cassettes, but with three or four hours of tape available, you should get all your performance on to one cassette.

Lighting could be a problem since there probably will not be sufficient light produced during the performance to give a clear recording.

You will have a better chance during the daytime when natural light plus artificial light will satisfy the camera's needs.

You could use video lights but these tend to be so strong that your young performers will find them difficult to cope with. With evening performances, why not video the daytime dress rehearsal?

Who is going to operate the camera? This problem was solved for us when two of our 11-year-olds volunteered to be video cameramen. The parent who was lending us the video camera kindly offered to give the two cameramen a crash course handling the camera, and they made a superb job of the dress rehearsal and two performances.

If the camera is portable and uses batteries, check the power input and recharge if necessary.

Selling the tapes

Assuming the recordings are of a good quality (which depends upon the recording machine, the quality of tape and the operator, as well as the performance itself), then you could make copies to sell. You would need firm orders in writing, with a promise to pay, before going ahead with making copies.

Check the copyright on works you perform being recorded. If the entire recording is of unpublished works, or if you own the copyright, then life is far simpler.

For sound-cassettes you will need to consider the printing for inset cards and possibly the sticky labels for the cassettes themselves. I would recommend going to a printing firm and obtaining quotations. Such firms would probably not be interested in an order of 20 or 30 and will tell you their minimum order.

Bulk copying

Firms who copy cassettes in bulk will also have minimum orders, but it is worth getting quotations, for the alternative is to copy each order one by one on a dual-cassette machine. Even a machine with high speed dubbing will take a considerable amount of time to copy 20 orders. You may even find a firm that will do a complete package.

With a video-recording, your costs will be higher and you will need to consider this before going ahead with a bulk copying order. Here again, firm orders are essential

Good quality recordings could be copied and sold.

before any copying is undertaken. There are firms who will do the copying for you and you may well find a firm that does a complete package, providing camera and operator as well as copying facilities.

The local teachers' centre or the authority's resource centre may have both cassette and video cassette copying facilities and may even be prepared to copy for you. They will probably be unimpressed with an order for 50, but could well oblige with a small order. You would need to provide the cassettes, but the charge will be much lower than a commercial firm, although you may have to wait longer for the finished products.

A photographic record

Photographs are one other way of recording the performance. However, many schools are against photography during a performance, as it distracts both the performers and the audience, particularly where flashlights are used.

Try to arrange for photographs to be taken at the costume parade or the dress rehearsal. Photographs taken during the project, including the dress rehearsal, could be displayed on the performance days and orders taken for prints.

Catering

You may consider providing refreshments for the children involved in the performance, or the audience, or both. Consider these questions:
● Are we charging for the refreshments? If so, how much?
● What refreshments shall we provide?
● Who's taking responsibility for the catering department?

● Who are the refreshments for?
● When will refreshments be served?
● Where will they be served?
● Have we sufficient equipment, cups, saucers etc?

Refreshments are a great excuse to socialise, and put faces to the parents of your pupils.

By charging a reasonable amount for

refreshments, you will also increase the chances of at least covering the outlay on the project.

What to provide

Most schools, I imagine, will provide tea, coffee, squash, biscuits and maybe crisps.

For a Christmas or other special festival production, you may consider appropriate refreshments: mince pies for Christmas productions and strawberries towards the end of the summer term. You could even organise a band of volunteer pickers to invade the local fruit farm early on performance day!

Buying and preparing

The cook and kitchen staff may be persuaded to oversee the catering, and they may even volunteer to organise the purchase of provisions and a job rota for serving. Otherwise, there are usually enough parents who will volunteer.

You may even decide to integrate this aspect within the project, and plan out and cost with the children a list of possible refreshments. With adult supervision, they could also prepare and cook the refreshments.

Where are the refreshments coming from? Will it all be bought from the cash-and-carry or local supermarket? Will you ask parents to make and donate? Will it be made in school? Remember to include in the overall budget, an amount to cover these provisions.

When and where?

Refreshments could be served during the interval, if there is one – this will depend upon the length of the performance. We usually reckon that up to an hour will not require an interval and so refreshments are served at the end.

Try to situate the refreshments in an area large enough to prepare and serve them and for people to chat.

Check that there are sufficient cups and saucers, plastic cups, plates, napkins, urns, teapots, kettles, trays and cutlery, and site your stall near the electric points.

The kitchen staff may be persuaded to help out.

Put someone in charge of washing up, and put out sufficient waste-bins to encourage people to be litter-conscious. Finally, make sure the refreshment area is well signposted and that the tariff board is prominently positioned.

Toilet facilities should also be well signposted. Check that toilets are clean and tidy and if staff toilets are being used, remind staff to remove all personal belongings from them – just in case.

121

Front-of-house

Safety

Like most school furniture, chairs are susceptible to a great deal of wear and tear and can become damaged and unsafe. Such chairs should not be used for the audience. The last thing your school (or local authority) wants is a claim for damages caused by an unsafe chair.

Some chairs are now designed to link, making whole sections or even a row rigid. This is a safety factor so that in the case of an emergency where the room has to be evacuated quickly, people will not be hampered or injured because of loose chairs. If your chairs are so designed, make sure that they are securely linked.

Emergency exits

You will be required to have emergency exits and these should be clearly identifiable to the audience throughout the performance. This may mean illuminating the signs, in which case check a few days before the performance that all bulbs, batteries and leads are working. Should a fire inspection take place and the fire officer is not satisfied with safety standards, your performance could be stopped. So check the regulations.

Having checked the emergency exit signs, make sure that they do direct people to an exit which will lead them quickly and safely outside the building. The outside doors should be unlocked or have opening bars on them. Have a word with the caretaker and remind him or her to lock the outside doors when everyone is off the premises after the performance.

Display copies of your school fire drill and make sure there is a fire extinguisher (in working order) in a handy position.

Always keep doorways clear and don't block an entrance by squeezing in those extra ten chairs.

Audience comfort

When the seating has been arranged, sit in different places and check the following:

● Sight lines – can you see the stage from any angle?
● Have you sufficient leg room?
● Can you reach your seat easily?
● Are the aisles in suitable places, and wide enough?
● Are the emergency exits visible and clearly marked from all positions?

Smoking and hygiene

Most parents will expect there to be no smoking throughout the school, so display 'no smoking' signs. The head may even mention this point in his or her opening words of welcome.

Between the dress rehearsal and the performance, the caretaker will be keen to carry out a final cleaning of the auditorium and you will need to arrange the best time to do this.

Audience comfort should be considered.

Keep the auditorium cool

Whatever the time of day or season, the auditorium will become quite hot with a large audience, so it is wise to open some windows before the performance begins. It may seem cold at first, but it does save a great deal of fuss later on, especially if there is no interval.

It can also help the performers to come into a cool, well ventilated auditorium. If they are nervous and excited, a warm, stuffy atmosphere can create problems. We experienced this at a dress rehearsal with windows closed, the audience generating lots of heat, the stage lights on and an excited chorus singing for all they were worth. Suddenly a lad on the front row of the chorus drifted gracefully from the vertical to the horizontal. Two members of staff were at the scene in seconds and whisked him out to fresh air before the rest of the chorus had realised what was happening. The windows were quickly opened, and he was back in position singing by the third number!

Tune the piano

If you are using a piano during the performance, arrange for it to be tuned as near to performance day as possible, and have it tuned in its performance position so that it doesn't have to be moved.

Check that all emergency doors are unlocked.

123

Decoration

What plans have you for decorating the auditorium? If the project has been an integral part of the curriculum, there will be material suitable for display. On the other hand you may decide to produce material in the last few days of the project to decorate the walls.

Flowers are always an attractive feature, and some schools have contacted their local parks or amenities departments who have supplied plants – often large and tropical – for the duration of the performances.

Insurance

For any school event where members of the public will be on the premises at the school's invitation, it is always prudent to check with the local authority and/or governors just what the insurance cover is. Are you, for instance, covered for equipment that you are borrowing from elsewhere? What is the amount of public liability cover?

Car-parking

Has the school got adequate car-parking facilities? Do you need car-park attendants directing the vehicles to allotted places? Remember to keep a clear way through to the main entrance in case emergency vehicles are called.

In the final week of the project, keep checking the school diary to make sure no visits or appointments have been planned which will interfere with the project. The arrival of the mobile bookshop is not the most welcome sight on dress rehearsal morning.

Backstage

Backstage could mean the kitchens, a corridor, a chair and PE store, the sides of the stage, or even behind the audience.

Assembly area

In any case, you need somewhere for children to change, to assemble before going on stage, and to return to when their performance is over.

If yours is an evening or weekend performance, take the children with their costumes to this area before the end of school, so that they know where to assemble, and you know where the costumes are!

Make a plan or a list of which rooms are being used and by whom.

Keep them quiet

If children have to wait before going on stage remind them to have a quiet game or comic or book with them. Try to provide paper, felts and crayons to keep them occupied.

Create a 'no noise zone' in the vicinity of the stage area, with signs designed by the children to remind them.

Now that you have reached this point in the book, you must be very close to the culmination of weeks of hard work and mental cruelty!

Just one more checklist and very soon you'll be putting on a performance.

Checklist

Check all the different aspects of the project regularly.

What form will advertising take?

Will advertising material be produced in school or out of school?

Is a poster competition being organised?

Will you need the help of the teachers' or resources centre?

Are you making badges or designing a project logo?

Have you budgeted for advertising and printing costs?

When will you start your advertising campaign?

Will you be producing tickets and/or programmes?

Are you charging an entrance fee?

Are you organising a retiring collection?

Will a recording (cassette/video) be made of the performance?

If so, do you need to check copyright?

What is the policy about photographs during the performance?

Are you considering sponsorship?

Are you sending out invitations and to whom?

What is the policy about reserved seats?

Will there be refreshments?

If so, who is organising them?

Will there be an interval?

Make sure children are kept occupied backstage.

What are the seating arrangements?

Have you checked fire/safety regulations?

Are there adequate, identifiable emergency exits?

What is the policy about smoking?

When is the final cleaning to take place?

Open windows and close curtains.

Does the piano need tuning?

Avoid arranging visits during the final week.

Will a display be mounted?

Which toilets are being used?

Is there adequate insurance cover?

Does car-parking need organising?

What facilities have you got backstage?

Where will the children change?

Where will they assemble?

Make a plan or list of backstage facilities.

Are there 'no noise zones'?

The performance and beyond

The performance and beyond

INTRODUCTION

Well, this is it! The performance is rapidly approaching!

The fact that you've reached this stage, and are satisfied that the performance will bring an audience away from the television and the warmth of their sitting rooms, means that it will go well.

Even if the dress rehearsal was totally 'underwhelming', and two of the main characters are suffering mild concussion having collided on the playground, the image of being hanged, drawn and quartered by the rest of the cast will soon dispel any fleeting thoughts of cancellation!

Final checks

The key to the success of the performance is your organisation, for you are the link between the many aspects of the project and the performance itself. How all the aspects come together will depend to a large degree on how you have kept a check on them over the past weeks, and how you have planned everybody's job during the performance.

Remember, you cannot be everywhere at once and a delegation of duties is vital to the smooth running of the performance.

Everyone who is involved needs to be clear of their role; it is a good idea to see everyone during the last couple of days and check that they know what they are doing. Print an information sheet of what has been discussed to jog their memories.

Timing

Leave sufficient time before the performance starts to prepare everyone and everything properly. The entire pre-performance preparation should be geared to starting promptly.

The finishing time is also important, especially for a morning performance if the room is used for dinners. Leave sufficient time to clear the props and staging so that dinners can go ahead as normal.

Similarly, with an afternoon performance, leave sufficient time beforehand to clear the room of dinner equipment and to allow for the dispersion of food odours and singing kitchen staff with tin and crockery accompaniment!

If the performance is taking place outside the normal school session times, ascertain who is responsible for unlocking and subsequently locking the school – the caretaker, the head or yourself.

An evening performance will give you a natural break between the end of the afternoon session and the time when children are due back. This gives the opportunity to finish off that prop or piece of costume, make notices for toilets and refreshments, and generally check that all is set for the arrival of the children and the audience.

Checklists

Make checklists of all the aspects that need to be checked before the performance starts.

Auditorium

seating neatly arranged
no litter
lights correctly positioned
stage curtains (if there are any) closed
props on stage as required
stage set for opening scene
band equipment ready (stands, music)
plugs/adaptors in position and working
room curtains closed
some windows open
emergency exits clearly signposted
emergency exit lights on
house lights on
reserved notices on seats if required

School entrance hall/ reception area

attractive display
press cuttings displayed
tickets/programmes available
money float if necessary
receptacles for retiring collection if required
sufficient space for wheelchairs

Get the children to make 'no noise zone' notices.

Outside school

car-parking space and an adult for car-parking duty if necessary
sufficient access to the building for emergency services
signs showing visitors how to get to the main entrance
sufficient outside lighting for evening performance

Front-of-house team

arrived and in position
know their duties
aware of emergency exits and emergency procedures
can direct members of audience to toilet and refreshment facilities
have displayed any notices/signs (including insurance disclaimer notices if necessary)
have access to first-aid kit

Backstage

all props accounted for and in position
costumes ready to be put on
adult supervisors in the right rooms before children arrive
all performers arrived
main characters present and have all they require
understudies available
'runners' in position (those children who have volunteered for backstage duties and who 'run' with messages, act as call-boy or do virtually anything to ensure the smooth running of the performance)
'no noise zone' notices displayed in obvious places
first-aid kit backstage (all adults must know where it is)

The need for checklists

I very much favour lists and checklists on occasions like these because, in the stressful atmosphere of a performance, the more mundane aspects are often passed by.

An incident involving a group of boys performing in a musical called *Charlie* demonstrates the need for careful checking.

The boys, who would be playing the parts of Scotsmen, were dressed in traditional tartan kilts and made a most dramatic entry, looking quite resplendent in their costumes.

Shortly after this entrance, they were required to sit down, at which point titters, then wholesome laughter burst forth from the audience (especially the front rows), for the 'Scots' had decided that the myth about wearing nothing underneath a kilt was true!

So next time you think of reserving seats on the front row for governors and invited guests, make sure you check all aspects of the costume!

Preparing the children

With half an hour to go before the performance begins, your role as director or producer is finished. You are redundant unless, of course, you have decided to take on another role, like stage manager, musical director, runner, tea-maker, scene changer, costume helper, make-up, last-minute props mender, or chief 'shusher' (that's the person who is continually have to say 'Shush, the audience will hear you!' So much for your 'no noise zone' posters!)

Boost confidence

A major part of your role now is to boost confidence and dispel nerves in every member of the project team, performer and helper alike.

As the children arrive, collect all the telegrams and messages of good luck and display them where they can easily be seen.

There may not be many telegrams, but often there will be some messages of good luck – even if it means writing one yourself,

just as you wrote that very complimentary article for the local press!

Now is the time to pin up those essential notices and posters in the area where the children assemble prior to going on stage, which are as eye-catching as possible and give the following messages:

Arrange the children in pairs or groups to help each other with costume, make-up and props.

Professional behaviour

Direct the children to the correct room or area, and remind them that the only time the audience should see or hear them is when they are performing – no wandering into the audience before the performance to say 'hello' to Gran, or peeping through curtains or scenery to see if Mum and Dad have arrived yet.

Avoid, at all costs, allowing a child to show her four-year-old brother behind the scenes.

All these unprofessional activities should have been explained and discussed with the children before performance day. It might be a performance by children, but you owe it to them and your audience to be as professional as possible and to create the best illusion of theatre – not destroy it before the performance begins.

Dealing with nerves

Once the children are busily involved in pre-performance activities, you must make a point of seeing all the team and saying to

them 'Break a leg!'

Whilst on your rounds, look calm, smile and encourage. It is very bad for morale to show even the slightest hint of being nervous, worried or panic-stricken.

The children will display their nerves in different behaviour patterns. Some will become very quiet and withdrawn, some will jabber on in an increasingly indecipherable way, while others may pace up and down or visit the toilet constantly. Your role is to find the right word or expression to calm every type of nervous behaviour.

Activities and games

You may decide to go through a few of the warm-up exercises mentioned in Chapter 2. This will help to calm the children by focusing their attention on someone and something else and dispelling some of their excess energy. It will also bring the team together and encourage children who may be feeling quite isolated and insecure.

Settle the children down once they are ready, and let them play quiet games or read, or even play a game of Hangman on the blackboard with them.

Arrange the children in pairs or small groups so that, while creating the 'team feeling', they can also check each other's costume, make-up and any other portable props they may need.

A cue for the start

The three-minute warning bell will cause an extra burst of excitement. Do check that if the school's internal bell system is used, the ring pattern is totally different from the fire alarm; otherwise you could find the entire cast lined up in the playground waiting for you to check them off!

A warning bell announcing that the performance is about to begin may seem unnecessary, but the audience needs to be made aware that the performance is imminent and that it's time to settle down. The head may venture on to the stage to welcome the audience and then signal the start. The welcome must be brief, sparing a thought for the children waiting backstage.

This is really the start of the performance, and should be cued by the stage manager once he or she is absolutely satisfied that all is ready and has checked with everyone backstage and front-of-house.

A last-minute check with the front-of-house team that all the audience is settled, doors are closed, aisles are clear and the house lights are ready to be switched off is essential.

Reserve a seat for the producer near the front.

Be prepared

You or a colleague who has been involved with the project from the beginning should have a seat reserved in the audience near the front. This I have found invaluable, for not only does it give the children a great confidence-boost, but it also means that if any emergency occurs on stage it can be dealt with immediately.

Check finally that your own personal 'first-aid kit' is at hand. This contains all the items that you might need during the performance to avert disasters:

safety pins,
Sellotape,
scissors,
string,
Blu-tack,
spare G-string (for violin repairs!),
tissues,
needle and cotton,
strong, quick-setting glue.

The list goes on and is added to through experience. And tucked away out of sight is that miniature bottle of brandy – purely for medicinal purposes, of course!

The welcome speech must be kept short.

The performance

Once the performance begins, all those pre-performance nerves, worries, anxieties and wobbly knees disappear, for things happen so quickly that you only have time to concentrate on what needs to be done at that very moment.

Audience reaction

Every performance is different. The performers will never give the same performance twice, and certainly audience reaction will be different. Moments when you thought the audience would be falling about in the aisles, pass by almost unnoticed, whilst lines that you thought held no chance of audience reaction are thoroughly enjoyed. (You should discuss this possibility with the children in rehearsal, and explain and practise the procedures.)

The children, without fail in my experience, give of their very best in a real performance; they slow their words down, sing out, act up just at the right moment and even react with the audience.

Arrange supervision

If some of the children do not need to stay until the end, make sure that they are

properly supervised and changed out of costume and make-up, and do not let them leave their allotted changing area until collected by a parent or designated person.

Some schools are happy for children to join their parents in the audience during the performance, whereas others supervise the children until an appropriate interval.

Encores

What about encores? Have you prepared a strategy, just in case?

Often a repeat of the final rousing chorus will be exactly right, but this needs practising with the children so that you're not left with half the cast on stage and the other half drifting off stage in a puzzled and confused way.

If your performance is a play without final chorus, decide upon the number of curtain calls, who takes them and in what order. The final bow should involve all the cast showing the audience that it really was a team effort.

In other performances, a curtain call will be inappropriate, but you still need to consider the ending so that the performance doesn't just fade leaving the audience wondering whether it's finished or not.

A vote of thanks

Will there be any speeches after the performance?

With so many people involved in the project, a vote of thanks (probably by the head) could be lengthy, so limit the thanks to general areas rather than individuals. Also, by naming individuals, someone always thinks they should have been mentioned and feels quite aggrieved to have been omitted.

Perhaps the three general areas to mention would be:
● thanks to everyone who has helped in any way towards this magnificent performance,
● thanks to you, the audience, for coming along and supporting us so well,
● but a very special thanks goes, of course, to the children.

. . . and beyond

Congratulations

Well, the performance has ended but you still can't relax.

After the children gave so much energy, concentration and pleasure, your first post-performance job must be to see all the children and congratulate and thank them.

They'll have lots to tell you about missed musical cues and how the beanstalk nearly collapsed, the squeaky clarinet that made the audience laugh and the fact that the audience were shouting for more at the end.

Other comments and anecdotes will come to light over a longer period – perhaps days, even weeks – and one or two impressions will stay with the children for a long time.

Clearing up

By the time you've had a word with all the children the auditorium may be ready to be tidied. Chairs need putting straight or maybe stacking if this was the final performance.

The stage may need to be 'struck' (taken down), but if there are other performances, set the stage for the opening scene.

Check the windows are all closed/locked and that the emergency lights are switched off. Check the electrics – all the lights need to be unplugged and made safe.

Any valuable equipment – music centres, projectors, instruments, tape/cassette-recorders and props – will need to be locked away safely.

Back down to earth!

When the last child has been collected, you and your equally exhausted colleagues might make it to the local hostelry . . . but not for too long, of course! Tomorrow's another school day and with six sets of work to mark and lessons to prepare, 9am will

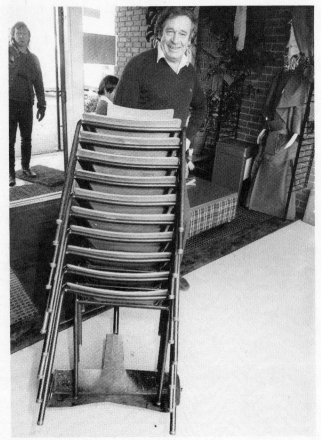

Chairs are stacked after the final performance.

soon arrive, and it's back to the routine.

Although the performance is behind you and school life is quickly returning to its former 'normality', it will not be forgotten, and you will no doubt at odd moments reflect upon its success.

More immediate, however, are the practicalities of tidying up all the loose ends and bringing the project to a conclusion.

Scripts and equipment

Scripts need collecting in and checking off on your list. All borrowed scripts should be returned and any that are missing, lost or in too poor a condition to return, must be paid for.

Set a date for all scripts and other equipment, costumes and props borrowed from school, to be returned. If any child fails to return equipment, you may decide to ask the child and/or parents to replace the item, pay for a replacement or make a donation towards it. Sometimes schools accept that some losses will occur and replacement costs will be borne out of the profits.

Equipment that has been borrowed or hired should be returned as soon as possible after the final performance. Hired equipment will be on a fixed period hire and so extra charges will be incurred if it is not returned by the agreed date. You will be charged for any breakages, and spotlight bulbs don't come cheap, so do take care in transportation.

Equipment borrowed by the school which has been damaged or broken during the project should be replaced, or at least the school should offer to make good such accidents. You may wish to borrow again!

Keep any equipment that evolved in school during the project and could be used again. You will need suitable storage areas for this to keep it reasonably tidy, dry and clean.

Treat the children

By this time, there may well be scores of congratulatory letters and messages arriving in school. Display them very prominently as soon as they arrive.

Check that all props are collected in, and set a date for costumes to be returned in good condition.

A party or treat for the children would be a tangible way of saying 'thank you' for all their efforts over the past few weeks.

It needn't be elaborate or consume a great deal of time to prepare. You might ask a group of parents to organise the catering side.

If you have recorded the performance, you could play back the recording at the party.

Of course, towards the end of such an occasion, be prepared for a chorus of 'What are we going to do next?'

This proves that the children have enjoyed the experience, and there's a greater chance of real learning if the task has been enjoyable.

Evaluating the project

There will be aspects of the project which you would approach differently next time. Mistakes become part of your experience and will hopefully be avoided in your next project. Similarly, because the next time will evolve from different circumstances and probably new personnel, other problems will arise, but there will also be many areas which will be more familiar to you and will not require so much deliberation and anxiety.

Aims and objectives

In evaluating and assessing the project you will need to turn back a few pages and look again at your aims and objectives.

How many have been achieved?

Has a start been made successfully on the long-term aims?

Which areas have been more successful than others?

What criteria will you use in assessing and evaluating?

The project seen as a whole

It is usually quite easy when going through an evaluating and assessing process to pick out isolated incidents that have succeeded or failed. This is especially so of things that didn't go quite right on the night.

However, it is the journey through the project which needs to be analysed, not merely the destination.

Much of the feedback and opinions concerning the project will refer to the performance, which has probably lasted an hour or even less. What fraction of the total time put into the project does this constitute?

Consult colleagues who have been responsible for certain areas of the project, and find out the successes and problems they have experienced.

137

The financial side of the project will tell its own success or failure story. Once a balance sheet is available, let parents know what any funds will be used for. This is also a good time to contact sponsors or local firms who've helped in any way, to inform them of the outcome and thank them for their support. It may even bring offers for your next project, in which case you'll have to consider putting on another performance!

But that is another story for another time and whilst you sit at your desk dreaming of that West End tour offer, your class is still waiting for an answer to their question: 'What are we doing in PE now the hall's free again?'

Treat the children to a party or outing to say 'thank you' for their efforts.

Checklist

The performance and beyond

Have you made pre-performance checklists?

Do all the helpers – backstage and front-of-house – know their jobs?

Who will act as stage manager?

Have you been able to hold a meeting of all helpers?

Is everyone costumed correctly?

For performances outside school time, who is locking and unlocking the premises?

Have you had a word with all the children, performers and helpers?

What activities have you organised for the waiting period?

How will the audience know that the performance is about to start?

Who will welcome the audience and signal the start of the performance?

Have you got your own 'first-aid kit' at hand?

What supervision have you arranged for the children who finish their part before the end?

What are the arrangements for encores?

How will the children leave the stage at the end?

Who will give the vote of thanks?

Have you organised a team of helpers for post-performance jobs?

Who is responsible for the money and where will it be kept?

Have all scripts been safely returned?

Has any damaged/lost equipment been replaced?

Has all borrowed equipment been returned?

Which equipment, if any, do you intend to store in school?

Have all the congratulatory messages been prominently displayed?

Is a party or treat being organised?

How will the project be evaluated or assessed?

Will you consider putting on another performance?

138

Resources

An Actor Prepares K Stanislavsky (Eyre Methuen *op*).

Bankside Book of Puppets H W Whanslaw (Darton *op*).

Complete Puppet Book L V Wall (Faber & Faber *op*).

Create Your Own Stage Lighting T Streader and J Williams (Bell & Hyman).

Create Your Own Stage Sets T Thomas (A & C Black).

Create Your Own Stage Props J Govier (A & C Black).

Designing a School Play P Chilver (Batsford *op*).

Directing in the Theatre H Morrison (A & C Black).

English Mummers and Their Plays A Brody (Routledge & Kegan Paul *op*).

English Ritual Drama E C Cawte *et al* (Folklore Society *op*).

Making Costumes for Plays Peters and Sutcliffe (Batsford *op*).

op Out of print, try libraries.

Once upon a Pantomime D Salberg (Cortney Publications *op*).

Practical Stage Make-Up P Perrotet (Studio Vista/Cassell and Collier Macmillan *op*).

Presenting and Producing a Pantomime R Marlow (Noda Pantomimes).

Puppetry Today H Binyon (Studio Vista/Cassell *op*).

Puppets B Snook (Dryad Press).

Puppet Theatre Handbook M Batchelder (Herbert Jenkins *op*).

Putting on a Play M Legat (Robert Hale).

School Play P Griffith (Batsford *op*).

Shadow Puppets O Blackham (Barrie & Rockcliff *op*).

Stage Management and Theatrecraft H Baker (J Garnet Miller).

Stage Properties: How to Make Them W Kenton (A & C Black).

Stanislavsky on the Art of the Stage K Stanislavsky (Faber & Faber).

Appendix A

Diary of a performance

The following is an extract from a diary kept during the stages of putting on a performance. The performance referred to is *Jackie and the BEANSTALK Game* (words by Elizabeth Chapman, music by Peter Morrell, published by Scholastic Publications in *Junior Education*, October 1986), and the diary follows the preparations between October and December 1986.

17 October

Distributed script to colleagues – each script in a smart, new folder!

24 October

Whole school in-service day; discussed putting on an end-of-term performance as part of the day's programme. Following decisions made:
● Go ahead with *Jackie and the BEANSTALK Game* (must have been the new folders that clinched it!).
● All children and staff to be involved.
● Dates and times of performances and dress rehearsals.
● Organise two casts – one for Monday evening and one for Tuesday evening.
● Staff involvement and areas of responsibility.
● Class and year-group areas of involvement.
● Ask the School Association to organise refreshments.
● Initial budget costs and sponsorship requirements.
(If copyright material is going to be used, you need, at this stage, to contact the publisher and/or copyright holder for permission to perform the work.)

25 October – 2 November

Half-term to contemplate decisions taken. Also a very useful time to work out:
● rehearsal schedule in weekly blocks,

● costume/lighting/scenery rehearsal dates,
● audition arrangements and criteria,
● band parts (written out),
● booking of guest artists,
● costume/lighting, scenery design.

3 November

Staff meeting – finalised previous decisions; discussed queries that had arisen. Organised pantomime 'notice-board'.

4 November

Introduced *Jackie* to whole school in two sessions. Audition lists put on notice-board; 24 hours given to sign up.

5–6 November

Saw all 124 who'd signed up (democracy does bring its problems); distributed audition pieces/songs; explained criteria and organisation of auditions.

7 November

Began auditions for main characters. Had hoped to complete today – no chance! Jane and Ann (colleagues) sat in on auditions.

10–12 November

Auditions – saw and heard every child who'd signed up; eventually made decisions. Duplicated list of main characters, etc; distributed to all staff/classes. Saw all auditionees to thank them.

13 November

Two casts sorted out initially; lists distributed to classes. Next week's rehearsal schedule organised – given to ancillary staff; pinned on notice-board. Duplicated scripts and numbered them.

14 November

Saw all main characters – gave out scripts (numbered) in folder; spoke to them of expectations, rehearsals, learning words by particular date. Made overhead projector sheets for chorus words. Initial information *re* performance sent to governors, guests, etc.

17 November

Rehearsals began (lunch-time, 12.05 to 12.55) – opening chorus and movements. 'Jackie's Theme' needed words – wrote them whilst Rose (colleague) organised children in opening movements. Band sounded promising. Wrote to local computer firm *re* sponsorship.

18 November

Chorus and characters – costume discussion with Sue and Jean (colleagues); made appeal for 'space hoppers' (chicken bodies)!

19 November

Karl and his gang, plus chorus – chorus area proving difficult to tier; asked first school for their stage blocks. Jane and Carole (colleagues) worked out dance routines and giant's castle scene – great!

20 November

Chorus, band, stage-hands. Saw Peter (colleague) about lighting schedule – more lights needed; enquire of local schools; follow up offer from local theatre.

21 November

Chorus, band, Karl and his gang. Discussed scenery with Ken, Brian, Geoff (colleagues) – contact local firms *re* cardboard boxes for scenery.

24 November

Chorus plus characters. Three weeks to go! Rehearsal schedule given to ancillary staff. Philippa and Claire (children) offered to take charge of notice-board – accepted gratefully! Spoke to all children about programme design (closing date – Friday).

25 November

Chorus, band, characters. Drew up props list. Acquired props box (plush affair on castors) – must inform art department one of their material boxes is missing!

26 November

Chorus, giant's castle, characters. Discussed sound with Sue (colleague) – need to borrow microphone and stand; all equipment in working order. Checked fuse box and maximum load for lights. Have we sufficient adaptors, extension leads, electric points?

27 November

Characters, band – music only. Checked make-up box – ugh! Buy in – see Sue about what we need.

28 November

Karl and gang, giant's castle. Collected programme designs. Send letter home *re* next week's after-school rehearsals for main characters only.

1 December

Two weeks to go! After-school rehearsals began – opening chorus, Karl and gang. Rehearsal schedule distributed to ancillary staff. Newsletter to parents with following information:
- costume requirements,
- dates, times of performances,
- organisation,
- Sunday rehearsal,
- mince-pie teams,
- reply slip for tickets.

2 December

Karl's gang, opening chorus; main characters after school. Children to write invitations to governors and guests. Checked costume progress with Sue and Jean.

3 December

Band plus main characters – songs only. Went through lighting schedule with Peter. How's the scenery coming along?

4 December

Karl's gang and chorus; Sue rehearsing main characters' musical items. Invited first school to dress rehearsals. Beanstalk coming along well; checked other props.

5 December

Karl's gang at break-time; giant's castle, chorus at lunch-time; main characters (Act 3 Scene 1) after school. Programme design chosen (Sarah Stones – 2M). Saw all cast – words to be learned off by heart by

Monday 8.

No reply yet *re* sponsorship – reminder needed? Timetable finished; classes with class teacher all next week and available for rehearsal. Distributed next week's rehearsal schedule.

8 December

One week to go, and counting! Hall available all day. Mornings – individual/small-group items; afternoons – whole cast; Act 1 – full run-through. Checked costume, lighting, props, scenery – all going well although I could get worried about the scenery being ready in time. Programme contents finalised; given to Pat (secretary) for typing/duplicating.

9 December

Act 2 run-through – afternoon. Rang local press *re* dates/times of dress rehearsal. Collected lighting batten from local school. Press-ganged more helpers for scenery. New make-up arrived. Reminded children of costume parade tomorrow. Started to allocate tickets/programmes. Moved equipment from hall.

10 December

Costume parade – amazingly, only three children still 'costumeless'; tremendous effort from children and parents; chickens could steal the show! Act 3 run-through – afternoon. Arranged lights during evening. Fixed carpet tiles to stage blocks – considerable difference in movement noise.

11 December

All musical items. Checked audience numbers – arranged chairs in hall. Tested emergency exit lights – bought new batteries. Discussed with staff jobs for Monday/Tuesday evenings. Tried to arrange video camera – not possible; organised cassette/tape for evening performances and operator. Scenery becoming a worry – especially how to operate giant's castle scene.

12 December

Full run-through with lights, props and scenery (well, some of it). Reminded first school of dress rehearsal times; checked school camera and film for dress rehearsal photos. Still no reply *re* sponsorship. Acquired receptacles for silver collection. Collected together all notices and signs – refreshments, toilets, etc. Still some last-minute props to make. Spoke to Jean (school cook) *re* refreshments; bought in mince-pie ingredients; contacted volunteer parents to make mince pies on Monday and Tuesday afternoons; arranged teams of children to help. Reminded children/staff of Sunday rehearsal.

14 December (Sunday)

Rehearsal with guest artists, drums, electric bass. Need to sort out microphone position. Continued with scenery – will paint be dry in time?

15 December

P-Day (P for performance)! Checked all cast at school. Mince-pie teams ready to go. Checked all departments – scenery almost there. Reminded children which rooms to use.

Dress rehearsal – didn't stop! Timed it – informed children of approximate finishing time. Made list of points, spoke to entire cast immediately afterwards – 'It'll be better tonight!' Press photographer arrived ten minutes after dress rehearsal finished. Tidied up chairs, stage, classrooms ready for tonight; stage set for opening chorus. Children took costumes to designated rooms just before end of afternoon school; reminded them of arrival time tonight.

7pm – house lights went down; spot on beanstalk; band started to play; children began to sing – magic!

16 December

A repeat of Monday but with the Tuesday cast. Scenery worked well today – all of it.

Appendix B

Copyright and performing rights

This appendix should help you to clarify your position with regard to copyright material and performing rights.

It is set out as a series of questions which are commonly asked, and answers which have been verified by the Performing Right Society Ltd the Mechanical Copright Protection Society and the Music Publishers Association.

At the end of the question-and-answer section you will find useful addresses.

What is copyright?

Copyright is both a form of ownership and a system of control linked specifically to the results of artistic and intellectual endeavour. It automatically comes into existence as soon as an original literary, dramatic, musical or artistic work has been created, provided it is written down or otherwise recorded in some material form.

Who is the copyright owner?

Copyright belongs initially to the creator of the protected work: ie author, composer, etc. In the music business certain rights, detailed later, are assigned to the PRS and others to music publishers.

What does the copyright owner control?

In the case of literary, dramatic or musical works, the copyright owner can control the following uses of the work:
a) reproducing the work in any material form,
b) performing the work in public,
c) publishing the work,
d) broadcasting the work,
e) including the work in a cable programme,
f) making any adaptation of the work,
g) doing, in relation to an adaptation of the work, any of the acts specified in relation to the work in paragraphs (a) to (e). (For

example, photocopying copyright material is generally illegal, and contravenes the Copyright Act of 1956, unless the permission of the copyright owner has been sought and granted. Even if your local education authority has taken out a licence to cover educational institutions for limited copying of books and periodicals without prior permission. Printed music, including the words, is specifically excluded from any such licence. Therefore, permission to copy printed music must always be sought from the copyright owner – usually the music publisher named at the foot of the page.)

How long does copyright protection last?

Normally, copyright protection lasts for the life of the creator plus 50 years thereafter, whilst a publisher's copyright in the typography lasts for 25 years from the publication of that edition.

Can a work be formally registered for copyright protection?

Evidence of authorship can be stored, although no registration or other formality is required to secure copyright protection.

How can a work be registered?

There are basically three methods:
1 Deposit a copy of the work with a responsible person, such as a bank manager or solicitor, and obtain a dated receipt.
2 Send the work via registered post to yourself, leaving it unopened on receipt. The composer should, for the sake of future reference, ensure that the title of the work is noted on the outside of the envelope.
3 A work can also be registered at Stationers Hall in London for a fee of £23 (correct at the time of publication and inclusive of VAT at 15%).

As copyright owner, can I sell the copyright?

It is not advisable. You would normally assign your copyright to a music publisher, subject to the rights of the PRS. A reputable publisher will publish your work at their expense, but if you are asked to contribute to publishing costs, beware. You should also exchange contracts and it is always wise to seek legal advice before signing.

What is the Performing Right Society?

The Performing Right Society (PRS) is an association of composers, authors and publishers of musical works, set up to administer, on behalf of its members, certain rights granted to them under copyright legislation.

What rights does PRS administer?

PRS administers:
- the right to perform a work in public,
- the right to broadcast a work,
- the right to include a work in a cable programme.

Collectively, these three separate rights are referred to as performing rights.

What types of performance are covered by PRS?

The rights administered by PRS cover non-dramatic performances of musical works by whatever means: eg live, tape-recorded, radio, TV, jukebox, etc.

What performances does PRS not cover?

PRS does not cover the performance of plays or sketches (or specially written music for plays or sketches), ballets, operas, musical plays or other dramatic musical works.

Who does administer these rights?

Permission to perform such works must be obtained from the publisher or (in the case of unpublished works) the author.

How do I obtain permission to perform copyright material?

It is the normal practice of PRS to issue annual licences to the proprietors of premises where music is publicly performed. If the premises in which you are to perform already holds a PRS licence, no further permission need be sought. However, if no licence is held, a permit may be obtained by the organiser of that one-off event.

How much is a PRS licence?

PRS royalty charges are calculated under a series of carefully devised tariffs according to the extent of music use and its circumstances.

For works not covered by PRS ('grand rights' works, such as musicals, operas etc), permission must be sought directly from the publisher, and payment will depend upon the work itself and the circumstances in which it is performed.

Will the local authority (or governing body in non-maintained schools) hold a licence?

Local authorities usually take out one PRS licence to cover all their premises, including schools. A phone call to PRS's Licensing General Department will confirm whether or not your school is covered.

Will I have to complete any form or returns?

If PRS requires programme details from you, you will be notified by them.

What should I do if I want to play records or cassettes during a performance?

Contact Phonographic Performance Ltd, who issue licences on behalf of the makers of sound-recordings to cover the public performance of sound-recordings. A PRS licence is still required.

What about photocopying?

Quite recently, the Copyright Licensing Agency (CLA) was set up to grant licences to local authorities, allowing schools to copy certain publications 'within clearly defined limits'. Check whether your authority has a licence. If so, your school will have a Licensed Copying User Guidelines document, which clearly explains the 'dos' and 'don'ts'. However, this licence does *not* cover printed music. Copyright printed music must not be photocopied for performance without written permission from the music publisher. Advice can be obtained from the MPA which has produced a booklet, *The Code of Fair Practice*, which gives specific guidelines to music users.

What is mechanical copyright?

Mechanical copyright is the right to record, usually on to disc or tape.

If I want to record a performance of copyright material, what permission do I need?

Permission to record copyright material must be obtained from the copyright holder *before* making a recording.

Will any fee be involved?

The Mechanical Copyright Protection Society (MCPS) administers agreements between music users and its members. It both collects and distributes royalties on mechanical reproductions.

If I use an overhead projector transparency to teach songs for a performance, do I need permission?

If the song is in copyright, you will need written permission from the copyright owner to reproduce it, and you must acknowledge them on the reproduction.

Sometimes I write new words to an existing tune. What is the copyright situation?

Again, you will need to seek the written permission of the publisher or copyright owner of the work concerned.

What are the legal consequences of infringing copyright?

Quite considerable, as Oakham School, Leicestershire and Wolverhampton Local Education Authority will confirm, since action was brought against them for copyright infringements involving the multitude copying of printed music.

Copyright is a complex area of legislation with much of the law related to the Copyright Act of 1956 – a time, of course, before the technological revolution produced such a plethora of reproducing and copying facilities.

Many copyright owners earn their living from their works, and rely on royalties for their livelihood. To infringe the copyright laws is to deny copyright owners what is legally theirs.

The golden rule is: always obtain permission from the copyright owner before copying, performing or recording, unless you and/or your school is covered by licence or other agreement.

Ignorance of the law will be no defence in court!

Useful addresses

Performing Right Society Ltd,
29/33 Berners Street,
London W1P 4AA; tel 01-580 5544.

Mechanical Copyright Protection Society
  Ltd,
Elgar House,
41 Streatham High Road,
London SW16 1ER; tel 01-769 4400.

Phonograph Performance Ltd,
Ganton House,
14-22 Ganton Street,
London W1V 1LB; tel 01-437 0311.

Stationers Hall,
Stationers Hall Court,
Ludgate Hill,
London EC4M 7DD; tel 01-248 2934.

Copyright Licensing Agency Ltd,
7 Ridgemount Street,
London WC1E 7AE; tel 01-580 9729.

Music Publishers' Association Ltd,
Kingsway House,
103 Kingsway,
London WC2B 6QX; tel 01-831 7591.

British Copyright Council,
Copyright House,
29/33 Berners Street,
London W1P 4AA; tel 01-580 5544.

British Theatre Association,
9 Fitzroy Square,
London W1P 6AE; tel 01-387 2666.
(Gives help with regard to copyright holders
of plays.)

Music Copyright Reform Group,
Copyright House,
29/33 Berners Street,
London W1P 4AA; tel 01-927 8322.
(An alliance of interested organisations
wishing to represent their members' views
with regard to the new Copyright Bill.)

Publishers Association,
19 Bedford Square,
London WC1B 3HJ; tel 01-580 6321.

Appendix C

Budget checklist

The following checklist will be useful when planning the financial side of your project. Not all of the items will be relevant to your performance, so you need to delete those which do not apply.

Scripts and/or music
    hiring or buying
Copyright fees
    scripts, music, recordings
Costumes
    materials and accessories for making
    hiring or buying
    wardrobes
Props (stage furniture and hand-held)
    hiring or buying
    materials for making
Lighting
    hiring or buying
    materials and equipment for making
Scenery
    materials for making
    transportation
Photocopying
    scripts and/or music
    rehearsal schedule
    job lists
    costume details
    newsletters
    posters and signs
Postage
    letters to parents

    newsletters
    invitations
Blank cassettes or tapes to record
    lines/songs
    performance
    sound effects
Make-up
Printing
    cassettes, programmes, tickets, posters, handbills, invitations, badges, T-shirts, inset cards and labels for cassettes
Staging
    hiring or buying
    materials for making and securing
    transportation
Sound equipment
    microphone and stand
    amplifier and speakers
    cable, adaptors, fuses
    cassette-recorder(s)
Video camera and cassettes
Camera and film
Refreshments
    making or buying
Transport for old people
Tuning piano
Lost or damaged equipment and scripts
    replacement costs
Party or treat for children
Material for decoration of school
Prize for lucky number

About the author

Peter Morrell, married with three children, was born in 1947 in Dewsbury, West Riding of Yorkshire. At four years old he began to learn the piano, and at the age of eight was performing in local concerts and providing the accompaniment at local pantomimes.

He decided to become a teacher when he was only 11 years old, and so at 18 he began his training at Worcester College of Education. Here he became involved with the operatic society, mime/dance productions and revues, the college orchestra and choir, and launching the Worcester Arts Festival.

His teaching career has taken him to public, junior and middle schools, and he is presently deputy head at Coten End Middle School in Warwick. During his time in Warwick, he founded the Warwick Schools Orchestra, and is now chairman of the Warwick Schools Music Association and a director of Warwick Arts Society, which organises the annual Warwick Arts Festival.

He has produced and co-produced many performances in schools, churches and theatres, and has written numerous songs and some musical productions. Publications include *Guy of Warwick*, a cantata for soloists, narrator, chorus and piano (published by Piper Publications), songs and articles in *Child Education* and *Junior Education* (published by Scholastic Publications), and songs included in a teaching programme, *In the Spirit We Belong*, published in Canada.

Guy of Warwick and other songs have been recorded and broadcast on BBC Radio, and he is presently 'composer-in-residence' for the Royal Leamington Spa Children's Choir, which has performed throughout England and in West Germany.

He is a member of the Performing Right Society and the Mechanical Copyright Protection Society.

Jackie and the BEANSTALK Game

Jackie and the BEANSTALK Game, by Elizabeth Chapman (words) and Peter Morrell (music), is a musical entertainment set firmly in the twentieth century, with a modern heroine and a computer in the main supporting role. We have included a good deal of dialogue, although there is room for adaptation and expansion for those who would like to add to the basic story.

The main characters are Jackie, her Mum, Dad and Gran, Karl and BEANSTALK (the computer). There are also small roles for a fairy and a man who delivers Jackie's cheque at the end. The scene at the beginning of Act 2 could be expanded to accommodate a large cast of children, since a number of pantomime or nursery rhyme characters appear from inside the computer to sing and dance. The range of well known pantomime and nursery rhyme characters is enormous, and in the case of nursery rhymes many children will already know the tunes well enough to sing and dance to.

The role of BEANSTALK is really that of a disembodied, computer-style voice, as the machine itself will need to be so constructed as to allow the pantomime characters to enter and exit from the stage through it. Other children can be part of the chorus in the group songs, or stage-hands, dressers, front-of-house helpers, and so on.

The costumes for the human characters should be fairly straightforward. Karl is a street boy, with a gang of hangers-on, who sing the backing to his songs, clicking their fingers to the music.

Both the script and the songs may be photocopied for use in schools.

Act 1

Scene 1: The living room of Jackie's home, Jackie is playing on her computer

Jackie's Theme

Jackie: Hey! Level 7! I'll zap those aliens, I'll get 'em this time!

(Arcade game sound effects.)

Oh no! The dreaded Black Blob! Come on! Move! Move! Oh no, it's got me again. That's the 45th time today! But I'll get there! I'll get there!

(Voices off-stage call her name as she continues playing.)

Mum: Oh there you are! I might have guessed! Jackie, are you listening to me?

(There's no response so she pulls out the plug.)

Jackie: Oh Mum! I'd've made it that time. I'm sure I know what I need to get rid of the Black Blob and get through the magic door!

Mum: Black Blobs! Magic doors! That's all you talk about these days. It's getting boring. When I was your age I had better things to do with my time than stare at a silly screen!

Jackie: (sullenly) They weren't invented then.

Mum: (taking no notice) I'd be out with my friends worrying about make-up and boys. (Jackie mimes accurately behind Mum's back.) Ooh I used to have such fun. I don't know what's wrong with children these days. They don't have any fun at all. It's all videos and computer games.

(Jackie tries stealthily to put the plug back in as Mum reminisces, but Dad comes in.)

Dad: No you don't, young lady!

Jackie: Please Dad.

Mum: (coming round) Well I can't stand here all day reminiscing. Now what did I come in for?

Dad: Have you asked her yet? It's about time that child got some fresh air. Look at her – all square-eyed and hunch-backed. What is the world coming to, eh Mum?

Song: A Parent's Lament

Mum: Why child why,
When others play outside
The games that children
    play,
Do you just sit all day, (sit all
    day)
By that machine (sit all day)
    by that machine?

Dad: Why child why,
Do you stay stuck in here,
Facing that flick'ring screen?
It makes me want to scream,
    (want to scream)
It makes me mad (makes
    him mad) I want to
    scream.

Mum: Why child why?
What do you see in there?
Why don't you wear a dress?
You look a frightful mess,
    (frightful mess)
Just comb your hair
    (frightful mess) do
    comb your hair.

Dad: Why child why?
Just leave it for a while.
What will they say in
    school?
You'll be an awful fool,
    (awful fool)
You'll get no job (what a
    fool) you'll get no job.

Mum: Please child please,
& Dad Just for your Mum and Dad,
Come for a little walk,
Stop while we try to talk,
    (try to talk)
We just give up. Just give
    up, we just give u-p.
    (sigh)

Jackie: Oh Mum!

Mum: Don't you 'Oh Mum' me. Now your Dad and I want you to go down to the supermarket. We'd go ourselves but Gran's got herself in a state again and she's popping round.

Dad: (in a low voice) Got more pop than popcorn, that woman.

Mum: Anyway here's the list and here's the money. Mind you don't lose it – it's the last we've got until pay day.

Jackie: Do I have to, Mum?

Dad: You do what your Mum says. The walk'll do you good.

Mum: Now off you go. There's a good girl.

(Jackie exits while her parents shake their heads mournfully.)

Jackie's Theme

Scene 2: The street. Jackie is trailing miserably along, kicking a stone. Karl is sitting on the side of the stage.

Karl: Hey kid! Mind where you're kicking that stone. Got some valuable gear 'ere.

Jackie: So what!

Karl: So I'm going to make me fortune. That's so what.

Jackie: Make your fortune with that load of old junk! Don't make me laugh.

Karl: You laugh if you like but I'm on the way up I am. Gonna make me fortune, probably end up a knight – others 'ave. Hey that sounds great. Sir Karl Kool. I can 'ear 'er now. Arise, Sir Karl.

Jackie: (giggling) More like the sack, Sir Karl! Anyway how are you going to make this fortune?

Karl: Well kid, just take a look at this.

(He pulls a cover off the pile of junk to reveal a large, rather cumbersome and unusual looking computer.)

Ta ra!

Jackie: I haven't seen one like that before. What make is it?

Karl: (tapping his nose sagely) Ah ha, that'd be telling, that would!

Jackie: Go on – you can trust me.

Karl: Well, perhaps I can. You're looking at the one and only BEANSTALK 25.

Jackie: It's a bit strange isn't it?

Karl: Madam, it's not only strange, it's miraculous. That machine, my dear, is magic. I wouldn't part with it for the world.

Jackie: Magic! I don't believe in that stuff.

Karl: Well you should. There's a lot of it around.

Jackie: Oh goodness, look at the time! I'd better not hang around or my Mum'll kill me. The shops are shut and I haven't got the shopping.

Karl: Never return empty handed.

Jackie: That's easy enough to say, but I don't see what I can do about it now.

151

Karl:	Take them a little surprise.
Jackie:	It'll be me that'll get the surprise.
Karl:	How much are you clutching in that hot, sweaty little hand?
Jackie:	Ten quid.
Karl:	Well for ten quid I might just be persuaded – might *just* I say – be persuaded to part with my machine here.
Jackie:	That old thing! Mum'd kill me!
Karl:	But when it has made your fortune child. What then? Then they'd sing a different tune!
Jackie:	I suppose it'd be an investment.
Karl:	More than an investment! Let me tell you.

Song: Karl's Song

Karl's gang	Super cool Karl is a really cool guy (cool) Super cool Karl is a really cool guy.
Karl:	If you wanna be cool Don't be nobody's fool. Be up top with the trend. Be a gold medal friend. See your name up in lights. If you wanna make the highest heights Then just listen to me Tell you how it will be.
Karl's gang	Super cool Karl, etc (as above)
Karl:	If you wanna be top, Be the pick of the crop, Then you're facing the man Who can give you the plan. Just you stick with me kid, Keep it hidden 'neath your curly lid, Then just hear what I say, You'll be rich in a day.
Karl's gang	Super cool Karl, etc (as above)

Karl:	I just know where it's at,
	So you stick with this cat.
	You'll be swimming in loot,
	In a gold lamé suit.
	Buy your folks old Buck
	    House,
	They'll be too shocked to
	    grumble and grouse.
	You can trust in me girl,
	Go on, give it a whirl!

Karl's gang	You can trust in him girl Go on, give it a whirl! Super cool Karl, etc (as above)

Jackie:	Will it really do all that? Quick, let me have it. I can't wait to tell Mum and Dad.

(Jackie hands over the money and trundles the machine away. Karl gloats over the money and exits whistling Karl's Song with Karl's Gang finger-clicking.)

Scene 3: Back in Jackie's living room. Mum, Dad and Gran are sitting chatting.

Gran:	And so I told her I did. I said if you can't find anything better to do than gossip, then I'm going.
Jackie:	(Jackie's voice interrupts). Mum! Dad! Look what I've got!
Mum:	My shopping I hope.
Jackie:	Look!
Mum:	Oh no!
Dad:	That child!
Gran:	Needs a good hiding!
Jackie:	But it's really great. It's magic! It's going to make our fortunes!
Dad:	Cost a fortune more like! Take it back where you got it from Jackie.
Mum:	But give me my shopping first.
Jackie:	Yes . . .well I can't really do that.
Mum:	And why not?
Jackie:	Well you see I haven't *actually* got it.
Dad:	You're not saying you haven't got the shopping.
Jackie:	Yes! No! I can explain. You see I met this bloke and he said I could have this and it's really magic and it only cost £10.
Mum:	My £10.
Dad:	This is the final straw. You're sent to do some shopping and you come back with a load of junk! Just you leave that there and straight to bed young lady! In the morning you take it and get our £10 back or else!
Jackie:	But Dad . . . .
Dad:	Bed!

(Jackie exits dispiritedly and Mum and Dad sit with their heads in their hands. Gran carries on knitting.)

Jackie's Theme

Act 2

Scene 1: Night-time in the sitting room. All is quiet. In a corner the BEANSTALK 25 is sitting quietly. Jackie creeps in.

Jackie's Theme

Jackie:	Good. They haven't thrown it out. I'll just have a little look to see what it can do. Now. Plug it in. Switch it on.
BSTALK:	(computer-type voice) Which game do you require?
Jackie:	Gee – a voice simulator!
BSTALK:	Less of your simulator please.
Jackie:	(astonished) Sorry. It's just that . . . I've never . . .
BSTALK:	Which game do you require?
Jackie:	Which would you recommend?
BSTALK:	(in disgust) Humans! They never know what they want! Well you asked for it!

(There are a lot of computer sound effects and from behind BEANSTALK emerge nursery rhyme/pantomime characters who dance a robotic-style dance and sing appropriate rhymes to improvised, electronic versions of the songs. At the end Karl emerges.)

Karl:	Hey man.
Jackie:	Where did you spring from?
Karl:	Here, there, everywhere. I get around.

153

Jackie: Do you know what's happening? This machine isn't like any I've seen before.

Karl: Didn't I tell you that man. Now you're in computerland. If you wanna get out you've got to play the game.

Final verse of Karl's Song

Karl's gang: Super cool Karl, etc.

Karl:
Kid just listen to me,
If you wanna break free,
You must join in the game,
Life's a risk you can't name.
Never said it would come,
Droppin' in your lap like a
 ripe plum.
If you want you must try,
Or just sit down and cry.

Karl's gang:
If you want you must try,
Or just sit down and cry.
Super cool Karl, etc.

(Karl's gang exits, finger-clicking.)

Jackie: Get out? Play the game? What are you talking about? I've just got to switch it off and . . .

(She leaps back from the switch as lights flash and noises come from the computer.)

BSTALK: I am operational. Do not break circuit. Warning. I am operational. Do not break circuit.

Jackie: I don't understand.

Karl: Let me put you in the picture man. You told BEANSTALK to choose a game.

Jackie: Yes but . . .

Karl: He chose his own game. The BEANSTALK Game. If you wanna get out you've gotta play it.

Jackie: Play it! Play what?

Karl: The BEANSTALK Game.

Jackie: How? Where are the rules?

Karl: (tapping the side of his nose) That's the problem.

Jackie: Great! Here I am stuck in a game I didn't want to play, with rules that don't exist. That's all I need! Whatever will Mum and Dad say?

Karl: Play it cool man. It's make or break time.

BSTALK: Excuse me for interrupting. The game must continue.

Karl: Sorry man. I'll be off. See you kid! (Exit.)

Jackie: Hey wait! You can't leave me here! Come back! (Shrugs her shoulders in resignation.) Well, I suppose I'd better play.

BSTALK: Press the second key on the left. You must collect eight feathers from the chickens' tails.

(Enter eight chickens with prominent tail feathers.)

If they peck you the game is over. Terminated.

Jackie: I'd better move.

(The chickens trace a regular path across the stage. Jackie dodges between them trying to get tail feathers. She has several close shaves, but eventually succeeds.)

Jackie: (collapsing in exhaustion) One, two, three, four, five, six, seven, eight. Eight feathers. I'd better keep them safely. I may need them later. What next? What now?

(Enter stage-hands carrying large shapes – triangles, squares, circles. They lay them on the stage like stepping stones.)

Jackie: I wish I'd never started this silly game. I wish I'd listened to Mum and Dad.

Song: I Wish I'd Listened

(Jackie and stage-hands)

Jackie: I wish I'd listened.
You cared, you told me.
But I never listened. I never listened.
You said I'd be sorry.
You're right, I'm wrong.
I should have listened.
I wish I'd listened.
Jackie never listened.

Stage-:
hands Jackie should have listened.
(repeat twice)
They're right. You're wrong.
You should have listened.

Jackie: I wish I'd listened.
You saw the problem,
But I never listened, I never listened.
I knew all the answers.
Me right. You wrong.
You knew the answers.
I wish I'd listened.

Stage-:
hands Jackie never listened.
(repeat as before)
You're right. They're wrong.
You knew the answers.

Jackie: I wish I'd listened.
I'm in this mess now,
'Cos I didn't listen. I didn't listen.

You've gone far away now.
You're gone. I'm here.
Why can't I listen?
I wish I'd listened.

Stage-:
hands Jackie never listened.
(repeat as before)
They're gone. You're here.
Why can't you listen?

Jackie: Please help me listen.
I've learnt a lot now.
Please help me to listen. I'll try to listen.
No one to hear from me,
Silence so loud.
No need to listen.
I wish I'd listened,
I wish I'd listened.

Stage-:
hands Jackie never listened.
(repeat as before)
Silence so loud.
You should have listened.
Please listen.

(Jackie ends sitting with her head in her hands. Stage-hands exit. Fairy enters.)

Fairy: You're beginning to learn, Jackie.
Jackie: Who are you? Where did you come from? Are you part of this silly game?
Fairy: In a manner of speaking.
BSTALK: The game must continue. The human must take the path to the giant's castle.

Jackie:	But what am I supposed to do?
Fairy:	In front of you is the path to the giant's castle. But only one way is safe. If you step on the wrong shape the game is ended. Take this magic stone to help you. Goodbye.

(Exit.)

Jackie:	I don't see how a stone will help.

(She tosses it between her hands)

Yes I do. If I throw it ahead of me it should show me the path. I hope it works. Here I go.

(She suits her actions to the words, jumping from shape to shape, always tossing the stone ahead of her.)

Jackie:	I seem to have done it. I bet it was all a trick. There's no magic path.

(She throws the stone back at the shapes. There's a loud bang.)

Oh well. I was wrong then.

(Enter Karl.)

Karl:	Hey man. You're doing great.
Jackie:	So far. But what comes next?
Karl:	Didn't I tell you it'd be great?
Jackie:	You did.
BSTALK:	The game must continue. The time available is being used up.
Jackie:	Time available! You didn't mention that!
BSTALK:	I cannot be held responsible for the actions of humans.
Karl:	Didn't I mention it? Too bad! It's easy man. You just have to get to the castle, find the hen that lays the golden egg, retrace your steps and there you are.
Jackie:	Where?
Karl:	Tucked up safe at home. No problems. No worries.

(Exit.)

Jackie:	But how much time have I got left? Too late – he's gone again. I wish I knew how much longer I have. Is it minutes or hours?
BSTALK:	Do you wish to terminate?
Jackie:	No. Let's play on. Lead me to the giant's castle.

(Exit.)

Jackie's Theme

156

Act 3
Scene 1: Inside the giant's castle. All is dark.

Jackie:	This is the tenth room I've been in and there's still no sign of the golden egg. I bet the wretched thing doesn't exist.
BSTALK:	Do you wish to terminate?
Jackie:	Is that all you can say? (mimicking) Do you wish to terminate? Just shut up will you!
BSTALK:	Unable to shut. I am not open. I repeat, I am not open.

(Enter Karl and Fairy.)

Karl:	I thought you'd be far away by now kid. Are you having problems? Perhaps my friend here can help?
Fairy:	Jackie, you have something with you that will help.
Jackie:	No I haven't. (Searches her pockets.) Pencil stub, paper tissue, sweet wrapper, sweet – a bit dusty but better than nothing. (Eats it.) Shell, pebble, eight feathers. No nothing useful.
Fairy:	Oh yes you have.

(Karl and Fairy conduct audience.)

Jackie:	Oh no I haven't.
Fairy:	Oh yes you have.
Jackie:	Haven't.
Fairy:	Have.
Jackie:	Haven't.
Fairy:	Have.
BSTALK:	Time is running out. Human unable to fulfil conditions of game. Time nearly over.
Jackie:	Not yet metal brain! Not yet! Golden egg – what lays an egg? A hen. What's special about a hen? It's a bird. What do birds have? Nests. Feathers. Feathers! That's it. Feathers! Tell me what to do with them.
Fairy:	Look over there.

(A large chicken is sitting at the side of the stage.)

Jackie:	I didn't notice that before.

(She goes over and examines it.)

I do believe. Yes. It's missing

some feathers. Perhaps these will fit.
(Fixes feathers on to chicken.)
        Yes.
(Chicken gets up to reveal golden egg.)

Song: Can it Be?
(Jackie, Fairy and Karl)

Jackie: Can it be?
        Here in front of me.
        Can't believe my eyes.
        I've nearly got my prize.
        I'm nearly there.
        I'm nearly there.

Jackie: Can it be
        That I really see
        Where my journey ends?
        What else the future sends,
        I've reached my goal,
        I've reached my goal.

Fairy: Yes for you
        Dreams can still come true.
        When you're far away,
        Suddenly comes the day,
        Dust turns to gold,
        Dust turns to gold.

Karl: It can be,
        If you wait and see.
        With me for a friend,
        Rainbows at journey's end.
        Just what I said,
        Just what I said.

All: We are here,
        That is very clear,
        In good company,
        Here where we planned to be.
        We're nearly there,
        We're nearly there.
        (repeat last two lines ad lib)

Fairy: Pick it up Jackie.
Karl: Hey man. That's really cool.
Jackie: (Picks up egg.) At last! Oh, oh I feel really ill. Really dizzy. The whole world's spinning. I can't stand up. I can't hold on.
(Everyone spins around, lights flash and there is a musical cacophony. When it stops Jackie is lying on stage alone.)
Jackie: Where am I? What happened? (Looks around.) Where is everyone? Where's my golden egg? Nothing! Nothing!

Scene 2: Back in the sitting room.

(Enter Mum and Dad.)
Mum: I'm glad to see you're up already.
Dad: Don't forget it's the tip for that load of old junk.
Mum: Is that the doorbell? Must be the milkman.
(Exit.)
Jackie: Must I Dad?
Mum: (re-entering) It's for you Jackie. Something about a computer program.
Jackie: A computer program?
(Looks at her hands and realises she's holding a disk/tape.)
        This one?

157

Man: It looks like the one young lady. If it's as good as I hear, it's worth a great deal of money.

Jackie: Money?

Man: Yes. I've brought along the cheque.

(He produces on outsize cheque, with a large sum of money written on it.)

It's just the first instalment, of course.

Mum: (examining cheque) *First instalment!*

Dad: Always said she was a talented kid.

Mum: Think of what we'll be able to buy!

Dad: Knew she'd go far with those computers of hers. It's the up and coming thing you know – technology – computer programming.

Jackie: Is that the doorbell?

Mum: (Exits and then enters with a crowd.) It's amazing how the news gets around!

Song: We've Heard the News

(the cast)

Small group: Dum de dum, etc.

All:
We've heard the news.
Can it be true?
Good luck has finally come
   to you.
We've heard the news
Broadcast around.
Computer fortune
   (computer fortune)
You've finally found.

Yes that's the news.
Champagne for all!
We're in the money so some
   for you all.
It's great the news,
We've hit the heights,
There is no mountain (there
   is no mountain)
Too high for our sights.

We're in the news,
TV and fame.
Make sure those papers can
   spell our name.
We are the news,
Smile at the lens.
Fans wait in line for (fans
   wait in line for)
Us waving their pens.

Spread round the news,
Failure no more.
Jackie's our winner, she's
   evened the score.
It's all good news,
Made it at last.
Problems will all be
   (problems will all be)
A thing of the past. Great
   news!

(Enter Karl quietly. The party continues at the back of the stage.)

Karl:	Wasn't I right kid?
Jackie:	I don't know how to thank you.
Karl:	Just hang on in there. That's thanks enough.
BSTALK:	No one ever thinks to thank me. I'm just a machine. You don't thank machines.
Jackie:	Thank you BEANSTALK. Nothing would have been possible without you.
BSTALK:	Nothing is possible. Logically imprecise. Processing information. Processing information.
Karl:	Come on kid. There's more people coming. Let's join the party!

Jackie's Theme

Finale

(an amalgam of the previous songs, sung by the whole cast as everyone gradually comes on stage)

Mum: & Dad	Smile child smile!
Dad:	We're proud your Mum and I.
Mum:	We always knew you'd try.
Mum: & Dad	You never made us cry (made us cry) You are the tops. You're the tops, our Jackie Po-ps!
Karl's: gang	Super cool Karl is a really cool guy (cool) Super cool Karl is a really cool guy.
Karl:	I never spun you no line, I was right all the time. You have made it all right With the peak in your sight, But if problems appear Then the way out should always be clear 'Cos if you've got a friend, It's all right in the end.
All:	Yes if you've got a friend, It's all right in the end.

All:	We are here, That is very clear, In good company. Here where we planned to be, And so goodnight! (sung six times)

Fairy:	(after first rendition of finale) And so our story's ended. Jackie's safe at home and it's time you all were too. Goodnight.

All:	We are here, That is very clear, In good company. Here where we planned to be. And so goodnight! And so goodnight! And so goodnight!

(ad lib repeats until all characters have exited, then a final 'And so goodnight!')

Jackie's Theme

A Parent's Lament

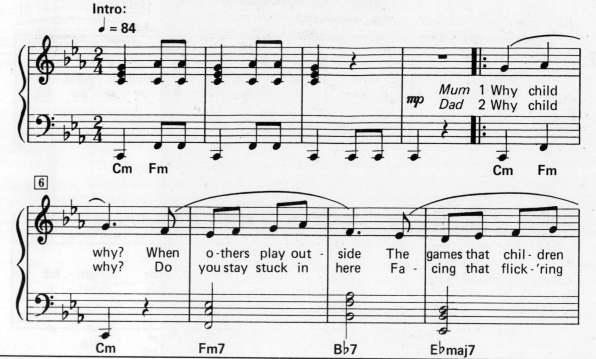

Karl's Song

I Wish I'd Listened

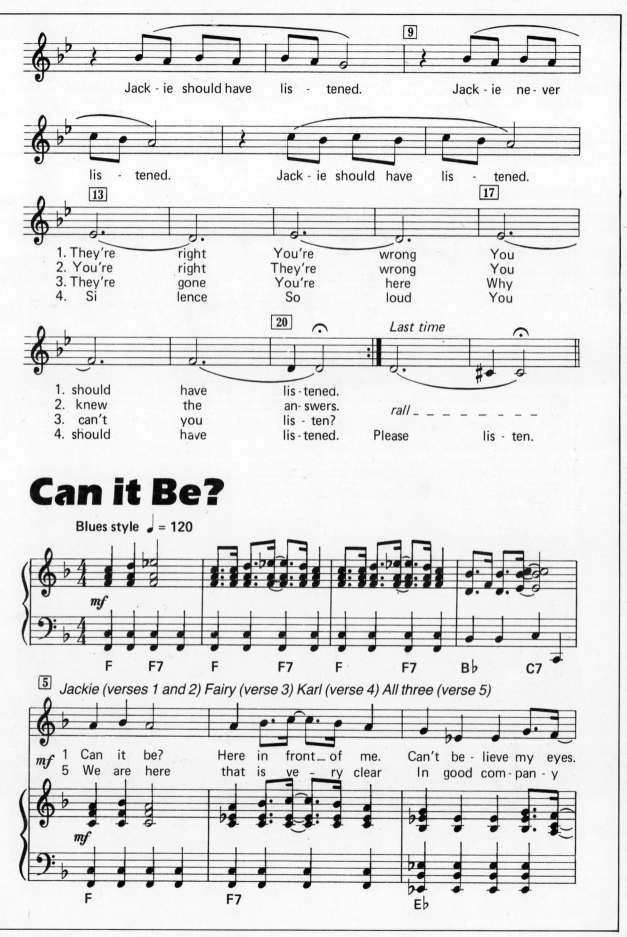

Jack - ie should have lis - tened. Jack - ie ne - ver

lis - tened. Jack - ie should have lis - tened.

1. They're   right   You're   wrong   You
2. You're   right   They're   wrong   You
3. They're   gone   You're   here   Why
4. Si   lence   So   loud   You

Last time

1. should   have   lis - tened.
2. knew   the   an - swers.
3. can't   you   lis - ten?   *rall _ _ _ _ _ _ _*
4. should   have   lis - tened.   Please   lis - ten.

Can it Be?

Blues style ♩ = 120

mf

F   F7   F   F7   F   F7   B♭   C7

Jackie (verses 1 and 2) Fairy (verse 3) Karl (verse 4) All three (verse 5)

mf
1 Can it be?   Here in front of me.   Can't be - lieve my eyes.
5 We are here   that is ve - ry clear   In good com - pan - y

mf

F   F7   E♭

167

We've Heard the News

♩ = 126 *Chorus*

mf (whistle)

G   Em   C   D7

5

f 1 We've heard the news. Can it be true?__ Good luck has fin-al-ly

8

come to you__ We've heard the news Broad-cast a-round__

mf

Bm   C   D7   Em

11

1 Com-pu-ter for-tune___ 2 Com-pu-ter for-tune_ ₁ } you've fin-al-ly found
                                               ²

f

Eb   D7

169

Finale

Karl

that is ve - ry clear, in good com - pan - y.

F7   Eb   F   F7

Here where we planned to be and so good-night

Eb   F

and so good - night And so good - night

Eb   F

It is advisable to contact the Performing
Right Society Ltd in respect of performing
any of the music.

and so good-night.___ And so good-night___

Eb   F Eb

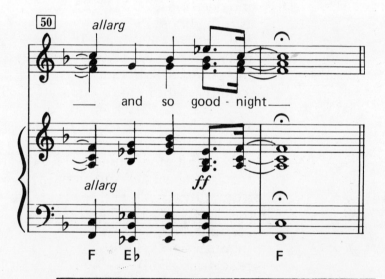

allarg

and so good-night___

allarg   *ff*

F Eb   F

After Fairy has said final
*'Goodnight', repeat from bar 36
to bar 47 then:-*

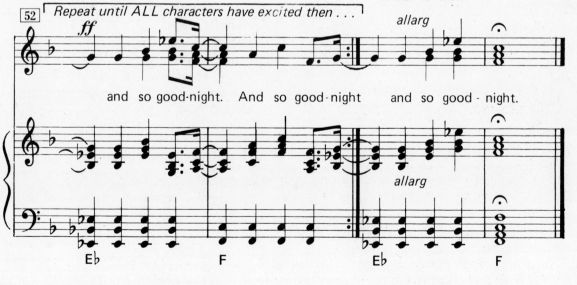

Repeat until ALL characters have exited then . . .

ff   *allarg*

and so good-night. And so good-night   and so good-night.

allarg

Eb   F   Eb   F

Index

A

Acting, 12, 25, 27, 54
  skills, 50, 51
Actors *see* Performers
Advertising, 15, 27, 108–13, 115, 116,
  125, 147
Alice in Wonderland Lewis Carroll, 5
Ancillary staff, 24, 29, 30, 117, 140, 141
Audibility, 49–50
Audience, 2, 25, 30, 47–9
  and advertising, 109, 112
  awareness, 50–1, 52, 53, 60
  comfort, 123, 138
  and dress rehearsal, 54, 55, 56
  for mummers' play, 6–7
  for musical, 12, 14, 16, 17, 18
  for pantomime, 18, 19, 20
  reaction, 51, 134, 135
  scenery, costume and props, 60, 65,
    67, 68, 72–6
  and staging, 81–5, 88–90, 92–5,
    97–100, 102, 104, 105
  tickets and invitations, 115, 118
Auditions, 15, 37–41, 57, 140
  see also Learning lines

B

Backcloths, 61, 64, 76, 84
Background, 64, 65, 66–7
Backstage, 88–9, 99, 105, 108, 124–5,
  130, 133, 138
Band, 17, 114, 130, 140, 141, 142
Behaviour, professional, 132
Briggs, Raymond, 5
Budget *see* Finance

C

Cabaret, 12
Call-boy, 130
Cantata, 13–14, 30
Car parking, 124, 125, 130
Cast, 57, 84, 128, 133, 140, 141, 142
  list, 35, 41, 67, 114
Casting, 38, 40–1, 45

Catering, 113, 117, 130, 137, 147
  organising, 27, 29, 37, 108, 120–1,
    125, 129, 140, 142
Cats, 12
Charlie and the Chocolate Factory
  Roald Dahl, 5
Charlotte's Web E B White, 4
Checklists, making of, 130–1
Children, 3, 22–3, 36, 38, 120, 121
  and advertising, 109, 111, 112, 114
  and decisions, 24–5, 27, 29, 30
  learning lines, 45–7, 56
  and musicals, 12, 13, 15–16, 17
  and pantomime, 18–19
  and puppets, 8–10
  scenery, costume and props, 60–1, 65,
    68, 69, 70, 71, 73, 74, 76
  and staging, 82, 83, 85, 86, 87, 104,
    105, 125
  tickets and programmes, 114, 117, 118
  see also Rehearsal, Auditions
Choreography, 27, 85, 141
Chorus, 22, 41, 109, 123, 140, 142
  costume, 67
  in musicals, 13, 14, 19
  rehearsals, 43, 51, 52–3, 141
  staging of, 84, 89, 92, 94
Cinderella, 18
Colleagues, 40, 136, 137, 140
  and planning, 36, 37
  and rehearsals, 43, 44, 57
  scenery, costume and props, 60, 61, 66,
    72, 73, 75
  and staging, 85, 95
Copyright, 19, 23, 28, 30, 35, 98, 105,
  119, 125, 140, 143–5, 147
Copyright Act (1956), 143, 145
Copyright Licensing Agency (CLA), 145
Costume, 22, 23, 111, 120, 134, 147
  casting and rehearsals, 40, 41, 43,
    44, 54, 56, 140
  checking, 129, 130–1, 133, 138, 142
  making, 59, 60, 61, 66–72, 76, 80, 141
  for musicals, 12, 14, 15, 16, 17, 20
  planning, 27, 28, 36

Acknowledgements

I should especially like to thank the following for their contributions to the production of this book:

Glenis Cole, Dave and Anne Hall, Sheila Hadfield, Wendy Helsby, Phil Litchfield, Richard Llewellyn, David Miller, David Walker and Joy Whitfield for permission to include their experiences from putting on numerous performances.

Elizabeth Chapman, whose richly worded scripts have subsequently become highly successful performances.

Sue Loveridge, whose expertise has created marvellous costumes and effects, including the masks and costumes on the cover of this book.

Lesley Funge and Jo Simpson for sharing their experiences of working with the Royal Opera House's 'Opera in schools' project.

Ken Teague, headteacher of Coten End Middle School, Warwick, for his staging and lighting ideas, and for his support and encouragement over many years of putting on performances at school.

All the staff (teaching and non-teaching), children and parents (past and present) of Coten End Middle School, for their enthusiasm and co-operation throughout many performances.

The headteachers, staff and children of the following schools for allowing their performances to be photographed: Bishops Tachbrook CE Combined School, nr Leamington Spa; Coten End First School, Warwick; Coten End Middle School, Warwick; Papworth Everard Community School, Cambridgeshire; St Mary & St John CE First School, Oxford.

Lyn Gray of the Performing Right Society, for her invaluable help and advice in compiling Appendix B on copyright.

Other Scholastic books

Bright Ideas titles

Previous titles in this series available are:

Bright Ideas Seasonal Activities
0 590 70831 7   £5.45

Bright Ideas Language Development
0 590 70834 1   £5.45

Bright Ideas Science
0 590 70833 3   £5.45

Bright Ideas Christmas Art and Craft
0 590 70832 5   £5.45

Bright Ideas Reading Activities
0 590 70535 0   £5.45

Bright Ideas Maths Activities
0 590 70534 2   £5.45

More Bright Ideas Christmas Art and Craft
0 590 70601 2   £5.45

Bright Ideas Classroom Management
0 590 70602 0   £5.45

Bright Ideas Games for PE
0 590 70690 X   £5.45

Bright Ideas Crafty Moneymakers
0 590 70689 6   £5.45

Bright Ideas Music
0 590 70700 0   £5.45

Bright Ideas Assemblies
0 590 70693 4   £5.45

Bright Ideas Writing
0 590 70701 9   £5.45

Bright Ideas Lifesavers
0 590 70694 2   £5.45

Bright Ideas Christmas Projects
0 590 70803 1   £5.45

Bright Ideas Spelling
0 590 70802 3   £5.45

Bright Ideas History
0 590 70804 X   £5.45

Set of any six titles   £27

Write to Scholastic Publications Ltd, Westfield Road, Southam, nr Leamington Spa, Warwickshire CV33 0JH. Enclose your remittance. Make cheques payable to Scholastic Publications Ltd.

Teacher Handbooks titles

Titles in this series available are:

Teacher Handbooks Reading
0 590 70691 8   £7.95

Teacher Handbooks Language Resources
0 590 70692 6   £7.95

Teach Handbooks Maths
0 590 70800 7   £7.95